# CAMBRIDGE LIBRARY COLLECTION

*Books of enduring scholarly value*

## Travel and Exploration

The history of travel writing dates back to the Bible, Caesar, the Vikings and the Crusaders, and its many themes include war, trade, science and recreation. Explorers from Columbus to Cook charted lands not previously visited by Western travellers, and were followed by merchants, missionaries, and colonists, who wrote accounts of their experiences. The development of steam power in the nineteenth century provided opportunities for increasing numbers of 'ordinary' people to travel further, more economically, and more safely, and resulted in great enthusiasm for travel writing among the reading public. Works included in this series range from first-hand descriptions of previously unrecorded places, to literary accounts of the strange habits of foreigners, to examples of the burgeoning numbers of guidebooks produced to satisfy the needs of a new kind of traveller - the tourist.

## Kinship Organisations and Group Marriage in Australia

N. W. Thomas (1868–1936) was one of the first government anthropologists of the colonial era and published one of the first studies of central African languages. This book, written in the early stages of his career, is a study of kinship structures in indigenous Australian peoples, and was first published as part of the Cambridge Archaeological and Ethnological Series in 1906. Thomas develops and defines fundamental anthropological concepts used today – such as consanguinity as a distinct term affecting descent, status and duties in a society –and emphasises the importance of seeing kinship terms as a social description, instead of merely describing biological relationships. His deconstruction of Lewis H. Morgan's theory of social evolution is also of interest for constructing a historiography of social anthropology. This volume contains views on ethnicity which were acceptable at the time this work was first published.

Cambridge University Press has long been a pioneer in the reissuing of out-of-print titles from its own backlist, producing digital reprints of books that are still sought after by scholars and students but could not be reprinted economically using traditional technology. The Cambridge Library Collection extends this activity to a wider range of books which are still of importance to researchers and professionals, either for the source material they contain, or as landmarks in the history of their academic discipline.

Drawing from the world-renowned collections in the Cambridge University Library, and guided by the advice of experts in each subject area, Cambridge University Press is using state-of-the-art scanning machines in its own Printing House to capture the content of each book selected for inclusion. The files are processed to give a consistently clear, crisp image, and the books finished to the high quality standard for which the Press is recognised around the world. The latest print-on-demand technology ensures that the books will remain available indefinitely, and that orders for single or multiple copies can quickly be supplied.

The Cambridge Library Collection will bring back to life books of enduring scholarly value (including out-of-copyright works originally issued by other publishers) across a wide range of disciplines in the humanities and social sciences and in science and technology.

# Kinship Organisations and Group Marriage in Australia

Northcote Whitridge Thomas

CAMBRIDGE UNIVERSITY PRESS

Cambridge, New York, Melbourne, Madrid, Cape Town, Singapore,
São Paolo, Delhi, Dubai, Tokyo, Mexico City

Published in the United States of America by Cambridge University Press, New York

www.cambridge.org
Information on this title: www.cambridge.org/9781108010511



This edition first published 1906
This digitally printed version 2010

ISBN 978-1-108-01051-1 Paperback

Cambridge Archaeological and Ethnological Series

# KINSHIP ORGANISATIONS

AND

# GROUP MARRIAGE

IN

# AUSTRALIA

# KINSHIP ORGANISATIONS

AND

# GROUP MARRIAGE

IN

# AUSTRALIA

BY

NORTHCOTE W. THOMAS, M.A.
Diplomé de l'École des Hautes-Études,
Corresponding Member of the Société d'Anthropologie de Paris, etc.

CAMBRIDGE:
at the University Press
1906

CAMBRIDGE UNIVERSITY PRESS WAREHOUSE,
C. F. CLAY, MANAGER,
London: FETTER LANE, E.C.
Glasgow: 50, WELLINGTON STREET.

Leipzig: F. A. BROCKHAUS.
New York: G. P. PUTNAM'S SONS.
Bombay and Calcutta: MACMILLAN AND CO., LTD.

DEDICATED

TO

MISS C. S. BURNE,

WHO FIRST GUIDED MY STEPS

INTO THE PATHS OF

ANTHROPOLOGY

# PREFACE.

IT is becoming an axiom in anthropology that what is needed is not discursive treatment of large subjects but the minute discussion of special themes, not a ranging at large over the peoples of the earth past and present, but a detailed examination of limited areas. This work I am undertaking for Australia, and in the present volume I deal briefly with some of the aspects of Australian kinship organisations, in the hope that a survey of our present knowledge may stimulate further research on the spot and help to throw more light on many difficult problems of primitive sociology.

We have still much to learn of the relations of the central tribes and their organisations to the less elaborately studied Anula and Mara. I have therefore passed over the questions discussed by Dr Durkheim. We have still more to learn as to the descent of the totem, the relation of totem-kin, class and phratry, and the like; totemism is therefore treated only incidentally in the present work, and lack of knowledge compels me to pass over many other interesting questions.

The present volume owes much to Mr Andrew Lang. He has read twice over both my typescript MS, and my proofs; in the detection of ambiguities and the removal of obscurities he has rendered my readers a greater service than any bald statement will convey; for his aid in the matter of terminology, for his criticisms of ideas already put forward, and for his many pregnant suggestions, but inadequately worked out in the present volume,

I am under the deepest obligations to him; and no mere formal expression of thanks will meet the case. I have been more than fortunate in securing aid from Mr Lang in a subject which he has made his own.

I do not for a moment suppose that the information here collected is exhaustive. If any one should be in a position to supplement or correct my facts or to enlighten me in any way as to the ideas and customs of the blacks I shall be obliged if he will tell me all he knows about them and their ways. Letters may be addressed to me c/o the Anthropological Institute, 3 Hanover Sq., W.

NORTHCOTE W. THOMAS.

BUNTINGFORD,
*Sept. 11th*, 1906.

# CONTENTS.



## CHAPTER I.

### INTRODUCTORY.



## CHAPTER II.

### DESCENT.



## CHAPTER III.

### DEFINITIONS AND HISTORY.



## CHAPTER IV.

### TABLES OF CLASSES, PHRATRIES, ETC.

## CHAPTER V.

### PHRATRY NAMES.



## CHAPTER VI.

### ORIGIN OF PHRATRIES.



## CHAPTER VII.

### CLASS NAMES.



## CHAPTER VIII.

### THEORIES OF THE ORIGIN OF CLASSES.



## CHAPTER IX.

### KINSHIP TERMS.



## CHAPTER X.

### TYPES OF SEXUAL UNIONS.



## CHAPTER XI.

### GROUP MARRIAGE AND MORGAN'S THEORIES.

## CHAPTER XII.

### GROUP MARRIAGE AND THE TERMS OF RELATIONSHIP.



## CHAPTER XIII.

### PIRRAURU.



## CHAPTER XIV.

### TEMPORARY UNIONS.



## APPENDIX.

### ANOMALOUS MARRIAGES.



---

## MAPS.



## TABLE.

# BIBLIOGRAPHY.


1. *Allgemeine Missionszeitschrift.* Gütersloh, 1874 etc., 8°.
2. *American Anthropologist.* Washington, 1888 etc., 8°.
3. *Année Sociologique.* Paris, 1898 etc., 8°.
4. *Archaeologia Americana.* Philadelphia, 1820 etc., 4°.
5. *Das Ausland.* Munich, 1828–1893, 4°.
6. *Bulletins of North Queensland Ethnography.* Brisbane, 1901 etc., fol.
7. BUNCE, D., *Australasiatic Reminiscences of Twenty-three Years Wanderings.* Melbourne, 1857, 8°.
8. *Colonial Magazine.* London, 1840–1842, 8°.
9. CUNOW, H., *Die Verwandtschaftsorganisationen der Australneger.* Leipzig, 1894, 8°.
10. CURR, E. M., *The Australian Race.* 4 vols., London, 1886, 8° and fol.
11. DAWSON, J., *Australian Aborigines.* Melbourne, 1881, 4°.
12. FISON, L. and HOWITT, A. W., *Kamilaroi and Kurnai.* Melbourne, 1880, 8°.
13. *Folklore.* London, 1892 etc., 8°.
14. *Fortnightly Review.* London, 1865–1889, 8°.
15. FRAZER, J. G., *Totemism.* Edinburgh, 1887, 8°.
16. GERSTAECKER, F., *Reisen von F. Gerstaecker.* 5 vols., Stuttgart, 1853–4, 8°.
17. *Globus.* Hildburghausen etc., 1863 etc., 4°.
18. GREY, Sir G., *Journals of Two Expeditions of Discovery in North-West and West Australia.* 2 vols., London, 1841, 8°.
19. GRIBBLE, J. B., *Black but Comely.* London, 1874, 8°.
20. HODGSON, C. P., *Reminiscences of Australia.* London, 1846, 12°.
21. HOWITT, A. W., *Native Tribes of South-East Australia.* London, 1904, 8°.
22. *Internationales Archiv für Ethnographie.* Leyden, 1888 etc., 4°.
23. *Journal of the Anthropological Institute.* London, 1871 sq., 8°.
24. *Journal of the Royal Geographical Society.* London, 1832–1880, 8°.
25. *Journal of the Royal Society of New South Wales.* Sydney, 1877 etc., 8°.
26. *Journals of Several Expeditions in West Australia.* London, 1833, 12°.
27. LAHONTAN, H. DE, *Voyages.* Amsterdam, 1705, 12°.
28. LANG, A. and ATKINSON, J., *Social Origins; Primal Law.* London, 1903, 8°.
29. LANG, A., *Secret of the Totem.* London, 1905, 8°.
30. LEICHARDT, F. W. L., *Journal of an Overland Expedition in Australia.* London, 1848, 8°.
31. LUMHOLTZ, C., *Among Cannibals.* London, 1889, 8°.
32. MACLENNAN, J. F., *Studies in Ancient History.* 2nd Series, London, 1886, 8°.

33. *Man.* London, 1901 sq., 8°.
34. MATHEW, J., *Eaglehawk and Crow.* London, 1898, 8°.
35. MATHEWS, R. H., *Ethnological Notes.* Sydney, 1905, 8°.
36. *Mitteilungen des Seminars für orientalische Sprachen.* Berlin, 1898 etc., 8°.
37. *Mitteilungen des Vereins für Erdkunde.* Halle, 1877–1892, 8°.
38. MOORE, G. F., *Descriptive Vocabulary of the Language in Common Use among the Aborigines of Western Australia.* London, 1842, 8°.
39. MORGAN, Lewis H., *Ancient Society.* New York, 1877, 8°.
40. NEW, C., *Travels.* London, 1854, 8°.
41. OWEN, Mary A., *The Musquakie Indians.* London, 1905, 8°.
42. PARKER, K. L., *The Euahlayi Tribe.* London, 1905, 8°.
43. PETRIE, Tom, *Reminiscences.* Brisbane, 1905, 8°.
44. *Proceedings of the American Philosophical Society.* Philadelphia, 1840 etc., 8°.
45. *Proceedings of the Australian Association for the Advancement of Science.* 1889 etc., 8°.
46. *Proceedings of the Royal Geographical Society of Australasia, Queensland Branch.* Brisbane, 1886 etc., 8°.
47. *Proceedings of the Royal Society of Queensland.* Brisbane, 1884 etc., 8°.
48. *Proceedings of the Royal Society of Victoria.* Melbourne, 1889 etc., 8°.
49. *Reports of the Cambridge University Expedition to Torres Straits.* Cambridge, 1903 etc., 4°.
50. ROTH, W. E., *Ethnological Studies.* Brisbane, 1898, 8°.
51. SCHÜRMANN, C. W., *Vocabulary of the Parnkalla Language.* Adelaide, 1844, 8°.
52. *Science of Man.* Sydney, 1898 etc., 4°.
53. *Smithsonian Contributions to Knowledge.* Washington, 1848 etc., 4°.
54. SPENCER, B. and GILLEN, F. J., *Native Tribes of Central Australasia.* London, 1898, 8°.
55. SPENCER, B. and GILLEN, F. J., *Northern Tribes of Central Australia.* London, 1904, 8°.
56. STOKES, J. L., *Discoveries in Australia.* 2 vols., London, 1846, 8°.
57. TAPLIN, G., *Folklore, Manners, Customs and Language of the South Australian Aborigines.* Adelaide, 1878, 8°.
58. *Transactions and Proceedings of the Royal Society of South Australia.* Adelaide, 1878 etc., 8°.
59. VAN GENNEP, A., *Mythes et Légendes.* Paris, 1906, 8°.
60. *West Australian.* Perth, 1886 etc., fol.
61. WESTERMARCK, E., *History of Human Marriage.* 3rd Edition, London, 1901, 8°.
62. *Wiener Medicinische Wochenschrift.* Vienna, 1851 etc., 4°.
63. WILSON, T. B., *Narrative of a Voyage round the World.* London, 1835, 8°.
64. *Zeitschrift für vergleichende Rechtswissenschaft.* Stuttgart, 1878 etc., 8°.

# INDEX TO ABBREVIATIONS.

# CHAPTER I.

## INTRODUCTORY.

Social organisation. Associations in the lower stages of culture. Consanguinity and Kinship. The Tribe. Kinship groups; totem kins; phratries.

THE passage from what is commonly termed savagery through barbarism to civilisation is marked by a change in the character of the associations which are almost everywhere a feature of human society. In the lower stages of culture, save among peoples whose organisation has perished under the pressure of foreign invasion or other external influences, man is found grouped into totem kins, intermarrying classes and similar organised bodies, and one of their most important characteristics is that membership of them depends on birth, not on the choice of the individual. In modern society, on the other hand, associations of this sort have entirely disappeared and man is grouped in voluntary societies, membership of which depends on his own choice.

It is true that the family, which exists in the lower stages of culture, though it is overshadowed by the other social phenomena, has persisted through all the manifold revolutions of society; especially in the stage of barbarism, its importance in some directions, such as the regulation of marriage, often forbidden within limits of consanguinity much wider than among ourselves, approaches the influence of the forms of natal association which it had supplanted. In the present day, however, if we set aside its economic and steadily diminishing ethical sides, it cannot be compared in importance with the territorial groupings on which state and municipal activities depend.

If the family is a persistent type the tribe may also be compared to the modern state; it is, in most parts of the world, no less territorial in its nature; membership of it does not depend among the Australians on any supposed descent from a common ancestor; and though residence plus possession of a common speech is mentioned by Howitt as the test of tribe, it is possible in Australia, under certain conditions[1], to pass from one tribe to another in such a way that we seem reduced to residence as the test of membership. This change of tribe takes place almost exclusively where tribes are friendly, so far as is known; and we may doubt whether it would be possible for a stranger to settle, without any rite of adoption, in the midst of a hostile or even of an unknown tribe; but this is clearly a matter of minor importance, if adoption is not, as in North America, an invariable element of the change of tribe. Although membership of a tribe is thus loosely determined, tribesmen feel themselves bound by ties of some kind to their fellow-tribesmen, as we shall see below, but in this they do not differ from the members of any modern state.

But in Australia the importance of the tribe, save from an economic point of view, as joint owner of the tribal land, is small compared with the part played in the lives of its members by the intratribal associations, whose influence is recognised without, as within the tribe. These associations are of two kinds in the lowest strata of human society; in each case membership is determined by birth and they may therefore be distinguished as *natal associations*. In the one case, the *kinship groups* such as totem kins, phratries, etc., an individual remains permanently in the association into which he is born, special cases apart, in which by adoption he passes out of it and joins another by means of a legal fiction[2]. The other kind of association, to which the name *age-grades* is applied, is composed of a series of grades, through which, concomitantly with the

[1] Howitt, *N. T.*, p. 225.

[2] Cf. Owen, *Musquakie Indians*, p. 122; Lahontan, *Voyages*, II, 203–4; Morgan, *Ancient Society*, p. 81.

performance of the rites of initiation obligatory on every male member of the community, each man passes in succession, until he attains the highest. In the rare cases where an individual fails to qualify for the grade into which his coevals pass, and remains in the grade of "youth" or even lower grades, he is by birth a member of one class and does not remain outside the age-grades altogether.

In the element of voluntary action lies the distinction between age-grades and *secret societies*, which are organised on identical or similar lines but depend for membership on ceremonies of initiation, alike in the lowest as in the highest grade. Such societies may be termed voluntary. The differentia between the natal and the voluntary association lies in the fact that in the former all are members of one or other grade, in the latter only such as have taken steps to gain admission, all others being simply non-members.

Although *primâ facie* all these forms of association are equally entitled to be classed as social organisations, the use of this term is limited in practice, at any rate as regards Australia, and is the accepted designation of the kinship form of natal associations only; for this limitation there is so far justification, that though they perhaps play a smaller part in the daily life of the people than the secret societies of some areas, with their club-houses and other features which determine the whole form of life, the kinship associations are normally regulative of marriage and thus exercise an influence in a field of their own.

Marriage prohibitions in the various races of mankind show an almost endless diversity of form; but all are based on considerations either of consanguinity or kinship or on a combination of the two. The distinction between *consanguinity* and *kinship* first demands attention; the former depends on birth, the latter on the law or custom of the community, and this distinction is all-important, especially in dealing with primitive peoples. With ourselves the two usually coincide, though even in civilised communities there are variations in this respect. Thus, according to the law of England, the father of an illegitimate child is not akin to it, though *ex hypothesi* there is a tie of blood between them. In England nothing short of an Act of Parliament can make them akin; but in Scotland the subsequent marriage of the father with the mother of the child changes the legal status of the latter and makes it of kin with its father. These two examples make it abundantly evident that kinship is with us a matter of law.

Among primitive peoples kinship occupies a similar position but with important differences. As with us, it is a sociological fact; custom, which has among them far more power than law among us, determines whether a man is of kin to his mother and her relatives alone, or to his father and father's relatives, or whether both sets of relatives are alike of kin to him. In the latter case, where parental kinship prevails, the limits of the kin are often determined by the facts of consanguinity. In the two former cases, where kinship is reckoned through males alone or through females alone, consanguinity has little or nothing to do with kinship, as will be shown more in detail below.

Kinship is sociological, consanguinity physiological; in thus stating the case we are concerned only with broad principles. In practice the idea of consanguinity is modified in two ways and a sociological element is introduced, which has gone far to obscure the difference between these two systems of laying the foundations of human society. In the first place, custom determines the limits within which consanguinity is supposed to exist; or, in other words, at what point the descendants of a given ancestor cease to be blood relations. In the second place erroneous physiological ideas modify the ideas held as to actually existing consanguine relations, as we conceive them. The latter peculiarity does not affect the enquiry to any extent; it merely limits the sphere within which consanguinity plays a part, side by side with kinship, in moulding social institutions. If an Australian tribe, for example, distinguishes the actual mother of a child from the other women who go by the same kinship name, they may or may not develop on parallel lines their ideas as to the relation of the child and his real father. Some relation will almost certainly be found to exist between them; but it by no means follows that it arises from any idea of consanguinity. In other communities potestas and not consanguinity is held to determine the relations of the husband of a woman to her offspring; and it is a matter for careful enquiry how far the same holds good in Australia, where the fact of fatherhood is in some cases asserted to be unrecognised by the natives. In speaking of consanguinity therefore, it must be made quite clear whether consanguinity according to native ideas or according to our own ideas is meant.

The customary limitations and extensions of consanguinity, on the other hand, cause more inconvenience. They are of course sometimes combined with the other kind, which we may term quasi-physiological, but with this combination we need not deal, as we are concerned to analyse only on broad lines the nature of these elements. Just as, with us, kinship and consanguinity largely coincide, so with primitive peoples are the kinship organisations immense, if one-sided, extensions of blood relationship, at all events in theory. In many parts of the world a totem kin traces its descent to a single male or female ancestor; and even where, as in Australia, this is not the case, blood brotherhood is expressly asserted of the totem kin[1].

Entry into the totem kin may often be gained by adoption, though not apparently in Australia, and the blood relationship thus becomes an artificial one and partakes, even if the initial assumption be accepted as true, far more of the nature of kinship than of consanguinity. In Australia, and possibly in other parts of the world, there is a further extension of natal kinship. Although the tribe is not regarded as descended from a single pair, its members are certainly reckoned as of kin to each other in some way; the situation may be summarised by saying that under one of the systems of kinship organisation (the two-phratry), half of the members of the tribe in a given generation are related to a given man, A, and the other half to his wife. More than one observer assures us that there is a solidarity about the tribe, which regards some, if not all other

[1] Two kinds of kinship are recognised in Australian tribes—(*a*) totem and (*b*) phratry or class—but the precise relationship of one to the other is far from clear. Nor is there much information as to what terms of kinship are used within the totem kin. It is certain that neither set of terms includes the other, for the totem kin extends beyond the tribe or may do so, and there is more than one in each phratry.

tribes as "wild blacks," though it may be on terms of friendship and alliance with certain neighbours, and feel itself united to them by a bond analogous to, though weaker than, that which holds its own members together.

If however a homonymous totem kin exists even in a hostile or absolutely unknown tribe, a member of it will be regarded, as we learn from Dr Howitt, as a brother. How this view is reconciled with the belief that the tribe in question is alien and in no way akin to that in which the other totem kin is found, is a question of some interest for which there appears to be no answer in the literature concerning the Australian aborigines.

Even if, therefore, we had reason to believe that all totem kins in a given tribe or group of tribes could make out a good case for their descent from single male or female ancestors, which is far from being the case, we should still have to recognise that kinship and not consanguinity is the proper term to apply to the relationship between members of the same group. For, as we have seen, it may be recruited from without in some cases, while in others, persons who are demonstrably not of the same blood, are regarded as totem-brethren by virtue of the common name.

Enough has now been said to make clear the difference between consanguinity and kinship and to exemplify the nature of some of the transitional forms. As we have seen, it is on considerations of either consanguinity or kinship that many marriage prohibitions are based.

Marriage prohibitions depend broadly on three kinds of considerations: (1) Kinship, intermarriage being forbidden to members of the same kinship group; a brief introductory sketch of the nature and distribution of kinship groups will be found below. (2) Locality. In New Guinea, parts of Australia, Melanesia, Africa, and possibly elsewhere, *local exogamy* is found. By this is meant that the resident in one place is bound to go outside his own group for a mate, and may perhaps be bound to seek a spouse in a specified locality. This kind of organisation is in Australia almost certainly an offshoot of kinship organisation (see p. 10), and is *primâ facie* due to the same cause in other areas. (3) (*a*) consanguinity, and (*b*) affinity. The first of these considerations is regulative of marriage even in Australia, where the influence of kinship organisations is in the main supreme in these matters. We learn from Roth and other authorities that blood cousins, children of own brother and sister, may not marry in North-West Central Queensland, although the kinship regulations designate them as the proper spouses one for the other. (*b*) Considerations of affinity, the relations set up by marriage, do not affect the status of the parties, so far as the legality of marriage is concerned, till a somewhat higher stage is reached.

In the present work we are concerned with kinship groups and the marriage regulations based on them. A kinship group, whether it be a totem kin, phratry, class, or other form of association, is a fraction of a tribe; and before we proceed to deal with kinship organisations, it will be necessary to say a few words on the nature of the tribe and the family. In Australia the tribe is a local aggregate, composed of friendly groups speaking the same language and owning corporately or individually the land to which the tribe lays claim. A change of tribe is effected by marriage plus removal, and possibly by simple residence; children belong to the tribe among which their parents reside. In the ordinary tribe each member seems to apply to every other member one or other of the kinship terms; and this no doubt accounts for the feeling of tribal solidarity already mentioned. There are however certain tribes in which the marriage regulations, as with the Urabunna, so split the intermarrying fractions, that the tribe is, as it were, divided into water-tight compartments; how far kinship terms are applied under these circumstances our information does not say.

The tribe is defined by American anthropologists as a union of hordes or clans for common defence under a chief. The American tribe differs in two respects, at least, from the Australian tribe; in the first place, marriage outside the tribe is exceptional in America and common in Australia; in the second place, the stranger gains entrance to the American tribe only by adoption; and we may probably add, thirdly, that the American tribe does not invariably lay claim to landed property or hunting rights.

The tribe is subdivided in various ways. In addition to the various forms of natal and other associations, there is, at any rate in Australia, a local organisation; the local group is often the owner of a portion of the tribal area. This local group again falls into a number of families (in the European sense), and the land is parcelled out among them in some cases, in others it may be the property of individuals. But there is a great lack of clearness with regard to the bodies or persons in whom landed property is vested. The composition of the local group varies according to the customs of residence after marriage, and the rules by which membership of the kinship organisation is determined. These two forces acting together may produce two types of local group: (1) the mixed group, in which persons of various kinship organisations are scattered at random; (2) the kin group, in which either all the males or all the females together with the children are members of one kinship organisation.

Save in the rare instances of non-exogamous kinship groups, the family necessarily contains one member, at least, whose kin is not the same as that of the remainder; this is either the husband or the wife, according as descent is reckoned in the female or the male line; where polygyny is practised, this unity may go no further than the phratry or the class, each wife being of a different totem kin.

Although it frequently happens that the children belong to the kin which through one of the parents or otherwise exercises the supreme authority in the family, it is far from being the case that there is invariable agreement between the principles on which kinship and authority are determined. Three main types of family may be distinguished: (1) patripotestal, (2) matripotestal, (*a*) direct, and (*b*) indirect, in which the authority is wielded by the father, mother, and mother's relatives, in particular her brothers, respectively. Innumerable transitional forms are found, some of which will be mentioned in the next chapter, which deals with the rule of descent by which membership of natal groups is determined.

Turning now to kinship organisations, we find that the most widely distributed type is the totem kin, in fact, if we except the Hottentots and a few other peoples among whom no trace of it is found, it is difficult to say where totemism has not at one time or another prevailed. It is found as a living cult to-day among the greater part of the aborigines of North and South America, in Australia, and among some of the Bantu populations of the southern half of Africa. In more or less recognisable forms it is found in other parts of Africa, New Guinea, India, and other parts of the world. In the ancient world its existence has been maintained for Rome (clan Valeria etc.), Greece, and Egypt, but the absence of information as to details of the social structure renders these theories uncertain.

Aberrant cases apart, totemism is understood to involve (1) the existence of a body of persons claiming kinship, who (2) stand in a certain relation to some object, usually an animal, and (3) do not marry within the kin.

Passing over the classes, which are peculiar to Australia and will be fully dealt with below, we come to a more comprehensive form of kinship organisation in the phratries. These are a grouping of the community in two or more exogamous divisions, between which the totem kins, where they exist, are distributed. The essential feature of a phratry is that it is exogamous; its members cannot ordinarily marry within it, and, where there are more than two phratries, there may exist rules limiting their choice to certain phratries[1].

This dual or other grouping of the kins is widely found in North America, the number of phratries ranging from two among the Tlinkits, Cayugas, Choctaws, and others, to ten among the Moquis of Arizona. As in Australia, the totem kins bearing the same eponymous animal as the phratry are usually, e.g. among the Tlinkits, found in the phratry in question. Exceptions to this rule are found among the Haida, where both eagle and raven are in the eagle phratry.

The Mohegan and Kutchin phratries call for special notice. The kins of the former are arranged in three groups: wolf, turtle, and turkey; and the first phratry includes quadrupeds, the second turtles of various kinds and the yellow eel, and the third birds. We find a parallel to these phratries in the groups

[1] For the facts see Frazer, *Totemism*, and cf. p. 31 *infra*.

of the Kutchin, but in the latter case our lack of knowledge of the tribe precludes us from saying whether totem kins exist among them, and, if so, how far the grouping is systematic; the Kutchin groups, according to one authority, are known by the generic names of birds, beasts, and fish. As a rule, however, no classification of kins is found, nor are the phratry names specially significant.

Dual grouping of the kins is also found in New Guinea, the Torres Straits Islands, and possibly among the ancient Arabs[1]; but evidence in the latter case has not been systematically dealt with.

Other peoples have a similar dichotomous organisation; but it is either not based on the totem kins or they have fallen into the background.

In various parts of Melanesia we find the people divided into two groups, each associated with a single totem or mythological personage, and sexual intercourse, whether marital or otherwise, is strictly forbidden between those of the same phratry[2]. In India the Todas have a similar organisation[3], and the Wanika in East Africa[4].

Customs of residence and descent affect the distribution of the phratries within the tribe, no less than the composition of the local group. With patrilineal descent they tend to occupy the tribal territory in such a way that each phratry becomes a local group. With the disappearance of phratry names this would be transformed into a local exogamous group, which is, however, indistinguishable from the local group of the same nature which is the result of the development of a totem kin under similar conditions.

As a rule kinship organisations descend in a given tribe either in the male line or in the female. Among the Ova-Herero, however, and other Bantu tribes, there are two kinds of organisation, one—the *eanda*—descending in female line and regulative of marriage, is clearly the totem kin; property remains

[1] MS. note from Dr Seligmann's unpublished *Report of Cook-Daniels Expedition*; *Camb. Univ. Torres Sts Exped.*, V, 172; *Man*, 1904, no. 18.

[2] *J. A. I.* XVIII, 282.

[3] *Man*, 1903, no. 97.

[4] New, *Travels*, p. 274.

in the *eanda*, and consequently descends to the sister's son. The other—the *oruzo*—descends in the male line; it is concerned with chieftainship and priesthood, which remain in the same *oruzo*, and the heir is the brother's son[1].

This dual rule of descent brings us face to face with the question of how membership of kinship groups is determined.

[1] *Ausland*, 1856, p. 45, 1882, p. 834; *Allg. Miss. Zts.* V, 354; *Zts. Vgl. Rechtswiss.* XIV, 295; *Mitt. Orient. Seminar*, III, 73, V, 109. The recent work of Irle is inaccurate and confused.

# CHAPTER II.

## DESCENT.

Descent of kinship, origin and primitive form. Matriliny in Australia. Relation to potestas, position of widow, etc. Change of rule of descent; relation to potestas, inheritance and local organisation.

IN discussions of the origin and evolution of kinship organisations, we are necessarily concerned not only with their forms but also with the rules of descent which regulate membership of them. Until recently the main questions at issue were twofold: (1) the priority or otherwise of female descent; (2) the causes of the transition from one form of descent to another. Of late the question has been raised whether in the beginning hereditary kinship groups existed at all, or whether membership was not rather determined by considerations of an entirely different order. Dr Frazer, who has enunciated this view, maintains that totemism rests on a primitive theory of conception, due to savage ignorance of the facts of procreation[1]. But his theory is based exclusively on the foundation of the beliefs of the Central Australians and seems to neglect more than one important point which goes to show that the Arunta have evolved their totemic system from the more ordinary hereditary form. Whether this be so or not, it is difficult to see how any idea of kinship could arise from such a condition of nescience. If we take the analogous case of the nagual or "individual totem" there seems to be no trace of any belief in the kinship of those who have the same animal as their nagual, but are otherwise bound by no tie of relationship. Yet if Dr Frazer's theory were correct, this is precisely what we ought to find.

[1] *Fortn. Rev.* Sept. 1905, cf. van Gennep, *Mythes et Légendes.*

This is, however, no reason for rejecting the general proposition that kinship, at its origin, was not hereditary; or, more exactly, that the beginnings of the kinship groups found at the present day may be traced back to a point at which the hereditary principle virtually disappears, although the bond of union and perhaps the totem name already existed. If, as suggested by Mr Lang, man was originally distributed in small communities, known by names which ultimately came to be those of the totem kins, we may suppose that daily association would not fail to bring about that sense of solidarity in its members which it is found to produce in more advanced communities. In the case of the tribe an even feebler bond, the possession of a common language, seems to give the tribesmen a sense of the unity of the tribe, though perhaps other explanations may be suggested, such as the possession in common of the tribal land, or the origin of the tribe from a single blood-related group. However this may be, it seems reasonable to look for one factor of the first bond of union in the influence of the daily and hourly association of group-mates. On the other hand, if, as Mr Lang supposes, the original group was a consanguine one, the claims of the factor of consanguinity and perhaps of foster brotherhood and motherhood cannot be neglected. It may be true, as Dr Frazer argues, that man was originally and still is in some cases ignorant of physiological facts. But all races of man and a great part of the rest of the animal kingdom show us the phenomena of parental affection, of care for offspring and sometimes of union for their defence. This does not, it may be noted, imply any predominance of the mother[1].

[1] It cannot be said that the ordinary theory of the development of kinship in the female line is satisfactory. The consanguine relation of mother and child does not appear to be a complete answer to the question why kinship—an entirely different thing—was reckoned through the mother; the alleged uncertainty of fatherhood is in the first place closely connected with an unproven stage of promiscuity and consequently hardly a *vera causa*, until further evidence of such a stage has been produced; and again among the Arunta, it is rather potestas than physical fatherhood which, on their theory, determines the kinship of the child so far as the class is concerned. For the primitive group therefore we cannot assert any predominant interest of the mother in the children nor yet admit that it would necessarily be important if it were shown to exist.

We may suppose that the idea of kinship or the recognition of consanguinity, whichever be the more correct term to apply to these far-off developments of the factors of human society, extended only by degrees beyond the limits of the group. First, perhaps, came the naming of the group, already, it may be, exogamous; then came the recognition of the fact that those members of it, viz. the women, who passed to community B after being born and having resided for years in community A, were in reality, in spite of their change of residence, still in fact the kin of community A; finally came the step of assigning to their children the group names which were retained by their mothers from the original natal groups. This brings us face to face with the first of the fundamental questions of descent, to which allusion has been made.

It is commonly assumed by students of primitive social organisation that matrilineal descent is the earlier and that it has everywhere preceded patrilineal descent; but the questions involved are highly complicated and it can hardly be said that the subject has been fully discussed.

Much of what has been said on the point has been vitiated by the introduction of foreign factors. Thus, the child belongs to the tribe of the father where the wife removes to the husband's local group or tribe. But though it may be taken as a mark of matrilineal institutions, often associated with matria potestas or its analogue the rule of the mother's brother, that the husband should remove and live with the wife, we are by no means entitled to say that the removal of the wife to the husband implies a different state of things. Customs of residence are no guide to the principles on which descent is regulated. Consequently it is entirely erroneous to import into the discussion with which we are concerned, viz. the rules by which *kinship* is determined, any considerations based on the rules by which membership of a *tribe* is settled.

Similarly, no proof of the existence of paternal authority in the family throws any light on the question of whether the children belong to the kin of the father rather than of the mother. Where the mother or mother's brother is the guardian, we are usually safe in assuming that descent is or has been until recently matrilineal. But from the undisputed existence of patria potestas no similar inference can be drawn.

Again, as will be shown below, not even the tie of blood between parent and child, confined though it may be in the opinion of the people whose institutions are in question, to a single parent, is an index to the way in which is determined the kinship organisation to which the child belongs.

It is therefore clear that the utmost discrimination is necessary in dealing with these questions; rules of descent must be kept apart from matters which indeed influence the evolution of the rules but are in no way decisive as to their form at any given moment.

Returning now to the alleged priority of matrilineal descent in determining the kinship organisation into which a child passes, it may be said that whereas evidences of the passage from female to male reckoning may be observed[1], there is virtually none of a change in the opposite direction. In other words, where kinship is reckoned in the female line, there is no ground for supposing that it was ever hereditary in any other way. On the other hand, where kinship is reckoned in the male line, it is frequently not only legitimate but necessary to conclude that it has succeeded a system of female kinship. But this clearly does not mean that female descent has in *all* cases preceded the reckoning of kinship through males. Patrilineal descent may have been directly evolved without the intermediate stage of reckoning through females.

The problem is probably insoluble. No decisive data are available, for the mere absence of traces of matrilineal descent does not necessarily prove more than that it had long been superseded by reckoning of kinship through males. All that can be said is that in the kinship organisations known to us female descent seems to have prevailed in the vast majority of cases and probably existed in the residual class of indeterminable examples.

With patria potestas it is, of course, different. There can be little doubt that it might and probably did develop in the absence

[1] *Année Sociologique* V, 104 sq.; VIII, 132 sq.; Tylor in *J. A. I.* XVIII, 245—272.

of kinship organisations and in a state of society where consanguinity is no real bond after the children have reached puberty. If therefore under such circumstances a kinship organisation were to come into existence, either independently or by transmission, it might well be that patrilineal principles prevailed from the first. But of such a case we have no knowledge. It may perhaps be questioned whether the actually existing peoples who appear to have no kinship organisations, such as the Hottentots, the Bushmen, the Veddahs and perhaps the Fuegians, are not in this state rather as a result of the break-up of their former organisation than because they have never evolved kinship groups. But our knowledge in these matters is lamentably small and the problem is not one which calls for discussion here.

The second fundamental problem relating to rules of descent is that of the cause of the transition from matrilineal to patrilineal descent. The subject needs to be discussed in detail for each particular area before general conclusions can be formulated; it is quite possible that the causes will be found to differ widely; for no general rule can be laid down as to the relations between matrilineal descent and other cultural conditions.

All that can be attempted here is an examination of the various elements in the problem so far as it affects Australia. To this may be prefixed a further discussion of the origin of matrilineal descent with especial reference to Australian conditions.

It is commonly assumed that in a pure matrilineal community, the husband removes to the wife's local group (matrilocal marriage), or if not that, that at any rate the authority in the family rests in the hands of the mother's brothers, who are also the heirs to the exclusion of the children. But of any such custom of removal there is but the very slenderest evidence in Australia. According to Howitt it occurs occasionally in Victoria and among the Dieri; among the Wakelbura it is done only if a man elopes with a betrothed woman and the man to whom she was betrothed dies; among the Kuinmurbura it seems to have been a recognised thing for a man who married a woman of another tribe to remove, but in this case he took no part in intertribal warfare[1]. In all these cases, the Kurnai excepted, descent is reckoned in the female line.

If however Dr Howitt's informant, who does not seem to have been particularly accurate in many cases, is to be relied on, the removal of the husband to the wife's group is also found among the patrilineal Maryborough tribes, though only if the woman belonged to a distant tribelet, whatever that may be[2]. To this information is added the statement that in such cases the husband joined his wife's tribe for purposes of hostilities also and that it has happened that a son has come into conflict with his father under these circumstances and endangered his life with full knowledge of what he was doing. There is, it is true, no definite statement to the effect that children in these tribes take their totems from the father, but we may assume that it is the case. If therefore the statement in question is accurate, it is a pretty clear proof of the break-up of the social system; for under no circumstances does the totem-kinsman, as a rule, violate the sacro-sanctity of his own flesh. It cannot therefore be argued that the fact of removal in the Maryborough tribes is any very strong evidence of the primitive nature of the custom. In the other tribes, on the other hand, it is distinctly stated that the practice prevails only when marriage takes place between members of two different tribes, and among the Wakelbura only exceptionally even when the wife is of an alien folk. Whatever else the custom proves in these cases, it certainly evidences the existence of friendly relations between the tribes in question; for if it were otherwise the man would hardly be disposed to give up the security of his own people for the perils of a strange community; on the other hand it is hardly likely that the man's tribe would allow him to pass over to the ranks of the strangers, nor would they view with equanimity the loss of effective fighting strength which would result from the fact that his children too would be numbered against them, not for them, if it came to hostilities. Of course these difficulties could be smoothed over by an exchange of husbands, corresponding to the commonly practised exchange of wives; but there is no suggestion of any practice of this sort. The custom is therefore clear evidence of

[1] Howitt, pp. 220, 225, 234, 248; cf. 159, 269.

[2] *ib.* p. 234.

fairly permanent friendly relations in the district in question; and it is plain that we cannot assume these to have existed in more primitive times. It is therefore difficult to see in what way the present day practices lend support to the theory that the original usage was for the husband to remove to his wife's group. For, be it noted, there is not a single case, unless we include the anomalous Kurnai, in which the husband removes to his wife's group within his own tribe; but clearly this is the custom to which the removal theory applies. So far, therefore, as Australia is concerned, the removal theory falls to the ground; it cannot of course be disproved, but we are not justified in assuming that matrilineal descent and matria potestas are due to a custom of removal.

Inasmuch as patrilocal[1] marriage involves descent of group and tribal property rights in the male line, it might appear that in rejecting the hypothesis of a prior stage of matrilocal marriage, we are involving ourselves in difficulties; for it is clearly not easy to see how descent could come to be reckoned through the mother, while property descended through the father. But it is obviously unnecessary in the first place to regard the individual rights of property as originating simultaneously or under the same conditions as the rules as to kinship or even communal property; there is nothing to show how long the present system of land tenure in Australia has held good, and it is clearly one which points to a certain growth of population; for if the local group were remote from their neighbours, there would be little need to encroach; moreover, the exact delimitation of territory now in practice is a thing of long growth.

Further consideration however shows that it is only by a confusion of thought that we can speak of land descending in the male line (that is, of course, in respect of group rights, not private property, to which we return later); strictly speaking the descent of landed property is neither in the male nor the female line but local. A man who removes to his wife's tribe is, so far as we can see, as truly part owner of the tribal land as if he were himself a member of the tribe by birth within its limits. The suggested difficulty, therefore, does not exist, and the conclusion as to removal customs holds good.

[1] P. 30 *infra*.

We may now examine the relation of matriliny to the seat of authority in the family. Questions of potestas naturally range themselves under more than one head. We have (1) the relation of the husband (*a*) to the wife and (*b*) to the children; (2) the relation of the mother to the children, and closely connected with this the influence of the mother's brother; finally (3) we have the position of the widow, a matter indeed more intimately connected with inheritance from a legal point of view but in Australia more closely connected with potestas than in countries where slavery is a recognised institution.

Small as is our information on Australian jurisprudence, it is certain that the husband enjoys practically unrestricted rights over the person of his wife, *pirrauru* and similar customs apart. He may at will lend her or hire her out to strangers; he may punish her infidelity, disobedience or awkwardness by chastisement, not stopping short of the infliction of spear or club wounds; he may even, according to Roth[1], go so far as to kill her and yet get off scot free, his only duty in such a case being to provide a sister for the brothers of his dead wife to kill in retaliation.

This custom suggests that the kin to which the woman belongs claim a certain property in her even after she is married, and this partial proprietorship naturally implies a slight protecting influence; for it would clearly not be in every case easy for the homicidal male to find a sister ready to go out and be killed as a set-off to his murdered wife. We should not, it is true, overlook the fact that the customs of the Pitta-Pitta differ from those of many of the Australian tribes, in that exchange of sisters is not practised. Otherwise it would be tempting to argue that this proprietorship in the women of their kin may go back to the time of Mr Lang's connubial groups and help to explain the reckoning of descent through females. For clearly, if a woman still belongs in a sense to the group she has left, so may her children belong to the same group, inasmuch as their relationship to her is, to us at any rate, unmistakeable. If any evidence could be produced for the widespread existence of the custom (found in various parts of the globe, though not, up to

[1] *Ethnological Studies*, p. 141.

the present, in Australia), according to which the widow and her children remove to her own district, some probability would be imparted to this hypothesis.

The ordinary rule as regards punishment inflicted by the husband on the wife seems to be that he may go any length short of doing her a mortal injury, without being liable to be called to account. The punishment of death however may only be inflicted for adultery and certain specified offences without incurring a blood-feud with the woman's relatives.

It is by no means improbable that under the influence of the custom of exchanging sisters there may be a tendency for the control of the kin in this respect to diminish; in fact the Boulia example is only explicable on this hypothesis. At the same time we cannot overlook the fact that elopement, or real marriage by capture, as distinguished from formal abduction, would, so far as we can see, have a similar effect, and the rise of the custom of exchange of sisters would in that case tend to re-establish rather than weaken the power of the woman's kin, at any rate in the first instance.

However this may be, the woman's kin exercises, *primâ facie*, some kind of protectorship. At the present day the kinship may be matrilineal or patrilineal without affecting their right. But if, before kinship was reckoned at all, this protectorship were exercised for the benefit of the children, we clearly have a possible cause of matriliny.

For a discussion of the question of the inheritance of the deceased's wife by his brother we have more facts at our disposal. As a matter of fact it is a not infrequent custom in Australia for the widow to pass to the deceased husband's brother[1]; or if she does not become his wife, he decides to whom she shall be allotted[2]. In no case do the woman's kin seem to have a voice in the selection of her new husband. On the whole therefore the proprietary rights found in the Boulia district seem to be the product of exceptional local conditions. If this is so, it is clear that in the matter of potestas the rights of the woman's kin are now absolutely restricted to protecting her from a death

[1] Howitt, pp. 193, 224, 227, 236.

[2] *ib.* p. 248, cf. 227.

which she has not according to native law deserved and to avenging such a death when it is inflicted by the husband.

The so-called levirate, or right of succession to the widow, is clearly of much importance, so far as questions of dominion are concerned; but as regards the problems of descent the evidence is less easily interpreted. It has sometimes been assumed that the succession of the brother and not the son is a mark of matriliny; but it is clear that where the right of appropriating the widow is concerned, this is very far from being the case, for the simple reason that the real matria potestas would put her at the disposal of the kin from whom she originally came; on the other hand, inasmuch as the son is naturally debarred from marrying his own mother or his tribal mother, who commonly belongs to a class into which he does not marry, there might easily arise in a purely patripotestal and patrilineal tribe a custom of handing over the widow to the father's brother.

On the whole however it seems simplest to regard the matter as one in which the rights are determined by no considerations of inheritance or descent but simply by the rule that the property in the woman remains vested in the body of purchasers. For it must be remembered that not only an own but also a tribal sister may be given in exchange for a wife. From this it follows that, theoretically at any rate, the contracting parties are corporations rather than individuals, and in this case the death of the individual on whose behalf the transaction has been effected does not extinguish the proprietary rights acquired by handing over a woman, standing in the relation of sister to the one corporation, in exchange for another woman standing in the relation of sister to the other corporation.

If this solution is correct, it is unnecessary to go into the complicated question of the relation of brother-inheritance to matriliny and patriliny. For it is by no means clear that it is an exemplification of the former rather than the latter principle. It may, of course, be argued that brothers succeed as children of the same mother; but against this must be set the fact that they are also children of the same father; for uncertain paternity can only be a *vera causa* where *pirrauru* and similar customs are found; and even here the pre-eminence of the primary husband might well be held to determine the legal paternity of the children, which is, of course, especially in Africa, a matter of potestas rather than procreation. However this may be, the position of the widow does not appear to invalidate the guardianship origin of matriliny.

We now turn to the question of why male tends to take the place of female descent. The possible factors are (1) authority in the family, (2) the rise of chieftainship and inheritance generally, and (3) the organisation of the family group. Of the authority of father or mother over the children, there is not much trace in Australia except in the most youthful period of the pre-adult life. It is for example exceptional for a parent to correct a child. As to who decides in cases of infanticide we have unfortunately too little information to be able to generalise. Only in one important step—that of betrothal—have we anything like adequate information, and the interrelations between rule of descent and potestas are found to be in this case sufficiently clear, though it is not clear on what principle it is decided *who* shall exercise the right.

Taking first tribes with matrilineal descent, we find that the Barkinji, the Wakelbura, the Dieri, and in some cases the Wollaroi, assign the right of betrothal to the mother or mother's brother[1]. In other cases, transitional forms, the father, his elder brother, or the girl's brothers decide, or else the parents or two of these persons jointly[2]. Among the Mukjarawaint the betrothal rested in part with the paternal grandparents[3]; it may be noted that the grandfather had to decide also whether a child should be brought up or killed. Among the Kuinmurbura it falls to the mother's brother's son or the father's sister's son, who is, apparently, entitled to marry the girl himself[4].

Turning now to tribes with male descent, we find that the father, his brother, or the parents, almost invariably make the decision[5]. Among the eight-class tribes, Spencer and Gillen assert in one place[6] that the mother's brother betroths a girl;

[1] Howitt, pp. 195, 221, 177, 217.
[2] *ib.* pp. 210, 227, 252, 216, 177, 260.
[3] *ib.* p. 243.
[4] *ib.* p. 219.
[5] *ib.* pp. 232, 257, 236.
[6] *Nor. Tr.* p. 603.

but this is contradicted in two other passages[1], and cannot be regarded as reliable.

On the whole therefore it appears that while there are some survivals of matria potestas into patrilineal descent, and in the matrilineal stage transitional forms are found, the right of betrothal tends to pass from the mother's to the father's side, when the rule of descent changes; but there is little to show how far a change in the right of betrothal tends to cause a change in the rule of descent.

A curious fact may be noted here, which goes far to demonstrate the absolutely heterogeneous nature of kinship and consanguinity, and suggests that descent is not reckoned in the female line on account of any supposed specially close connection between the mother and her offspring. Of the four tribes among which, according to Howitt, the child is regarded as the offspring of the father alone[2], the mother being only its nurse, two, the Yuin and Kulin, have male descent; two, however, the Wolgal and Tatathi, have female descent, and among the latter, in addition, the right of betrothal lies with the mother or mother's brother.

On the whole, therefore, it may be said that no questions of potestas seem to have exercised any influence in bringing about the transition from matrilineal to patrilineal descent. It does not appear necessary, therefore, to do more than allude in passing to a fact which may well have had something to do with the decay of matria potestas, at any rate, so far as the mother's brother is concerned, even if it did not actively hasten the coming of patria potestas. This fact is the considerable size of the area over which, with the rise of the so-called nations, it is possible to select a wife. The more remote geographically the mother's relatives, the less their influence. Allowance must of course be made for the opportunities of discussion afforded by the great gatherings of the tribes; but the wider area of bride-choice must have shaken the authority of the brother.

It has been remarked above that there is no well-established case of the right of betrothal being assigned on patrilineal prin-

[1] *ib.* pp. 77 n., 114.

[2] Howitt, pp. 263, 255, 198, 195.

ciples in a matrilineal tribe. The influence of the father's brother is not necessarily a mark of patrilineal tendencies, except in so far as all patria potestas is such. That the elder brother has authority in this case is no more decisive than that the elder brother has authority in cases of betrothal; it is no more an exemplification of the simple patria potestas, which has already been shown to be universal and under but slight limitations so far as the wife is concerned. From the point of view of potestas, it is a great advance that the father should be able to dispose of his own daughter in marriage; but if we may judge by the survival of matria potestas into patriliny, the cases of patria potestas under matriliny cannot have exercised an important influence in bringing about a change in the rule of descent.

The case of the power of the girl's own brother is somewhat different. *Primâ facie* it appears to owe its origin to the fact that it is the brothers who are mainly interested in the transaction, inasmuch as it is to them that wives come in exchange for the sisters given in marriage. Consequently we cannot, as has already been the case with the so-called levirate, assign the practice definitely either to matripotestal or patripotestal customs, for father's and mother's authority are alike overruled.

It has already been stated that we have but few data for estimating the influence of the right of betrothal on the rule of descent. Clearly the father has little to gain from the fact that his daughter follows him rather than the mother, when the inevitable effect of the marriage regulations is to make her children of the phratry and totem of her husband, and consequently to make them of a different phratry and totem from her father. Under matriliny on the other hand there is nothing to prevent the grandchildren from being of the same totem as the grandfather, and they are necessarily of the same class in a four-class tribe. If considerations with regard to the phratry and totem of the grandchildren played any part in bringing about a change in the rule of descent, this must have been based on a review of the changes that would be brought about in the position of the son's and not the daughter's offspring. But this is unlikely.

But on the other hand the father's disposal of the daughter's hand is indirectly a means of increasing his influence both with his son and in general. If the son gains his wife by an exchange of sisters, the father's authority is obviously increased. But we do not know how far this factor of the right of betrothal has operated.

Turning now to questions of inheritance, we find that properly speaking the hereditary chief is unknown in Australia. There is a tendency for the son of the tribal headman to succeed his father, but it is subject to exceptions. Moreover, it is by no means a universal rule for the tribe to have an over-headman; it may be ruled by the council of district headmen. In any case the influence of the quasi-hereditary character of the over-headmanship upon the rule of descent cannot but have been comparatively slight.

It is, on the other hand, usual for the local group and the totem kin to have headmen. In the case of the latter, age is often the qualification, as among the Dieri[1]; in such cases there is no possible effect on the rule of succession. But among some of the Victorian tribes with matrilineal descent the rule is for the son to follow the father in the headmanship[2]; and the same is the case, as we should expect, among the patrilineal eight-class tribes[3]. The most important tribe in which hereditary headmanship is combined with female descent is the Wiradjeri[4]; their neighbours, the Kamilaroi, showed marked respect to the son of a headman, if he possessed ability, though they did not, apparently, make him his father's successor[5].

On the whole, then, we cannot assign much weight to this element in the list of possible causes of the transition.

Of inheritance of chattels or land and fixtures we know little. From Spencer and Gillen we learn that among the Warramunga the mother's brother, or daughter's husband, succeeds to the boomerangs, and other moveable property[6]. Among the Kulin and the Kurnai inheritance in the male line seems to have been the rule. In the Adelaide district, as we learn from Gerstaecker[7], individual property in land was known; it descended in the

[1] Howitt, p. 298.
[2] *ib.* pp. 306, 308 sq.
[3] *Nor. Tr.* p. 23.
[4] Howitt, p. 303.
[5] *ib.* p. 302.
[6] *Nor. Tr.* p. 524.
[7] *Reisen.* IV, 347.

male line. Among the Turribul there was individual property in *bunya-bunya* trees; these too devolved from father to son[1].

On the other hand on the Bloomfield property in zamia nut grounds has vested in women and descends from mother to daughter[2]; but in this remarkable variant we see, of course, not the influence of the mother's kin, but female influence or rather the right of females to the produce of their labour. In respect of other property, inheritance in North Queensland is in the male line, for it descends to blood brothers and remains in the same exogamous group from generation to generation.

This brings us to the question of the part played by the local group in causing the change from female to male descent. Under ordinary circumstances, with female descent, the local group is made up of persons of different phratries and totems; in any case, just as the phratry and totem of the members of the individual family change from generation to generation, the complexion of the local group is liable to be completely changed; though in practice the changes in one direction are no doubt counterbalanced by changes in the other, so that the net result may be nil, when the original differences were small. But we cannot suppose that the group was often evenly balanced; and a change in the rule of descent would in that case have important results for the local group and in any case for the individual family.

The importance of the difference in the constitution of the local group under descent in the male line is seen when we reflect that in the normal tribe the totem kin is practically the unit for many purposes. If, for example, an emu man has killed, let us say, an iguana man, it is the duty of the iguana men to avenge the death of their kinsman. Their vengeance need not, however, fall on the original perpetrator of the deed; according to the rules of savage justice all the emu men are equally responsible with the culprit; consequently it suffices to kill the first emu person whom they can find. Conversely, those to whom an emu man looks for defence, when he is attacked, or assistance, when he wishes to abduct a wife or anything of that sort, are his fellow emu

[1] *Petrie's Reminiscences*, p. 117.

[2] *N. Q. Ethn. Bull.* VIII.

men. It is therefore clear that the rule of male descent gives far greater security to the members of a local group; for they are surrounded by kinsmen. Under the rule of female descent, on the other hand, they probably have some kinsmen in the same group but equally a considerable number of members of other totem kins.

Self-interest therefore, no less than the natural sympathy between fathers and children, as well as between members of the same group (quite apart from forays and fighting), must have tended to bring about a change in the laws of descent.

The late Major J. W. Powell has already described the transition from matria potestas to patria potestas among the Pueblo peoples. He put it down to economic conditions, which lead the groups to scatter, each under the headship of a male, who is also the husband; this naturally resulted in a weakening of the influence of the mother's brother. It is, however, less clear that it would bring about the decay of the power of the mother herself, which in Australian tribes, at any rate, seems to be independent of the support she obtains from her male relatives.

In Australia, as we have seen, the change from matria to patria potestas had but little influence in bringing about a change in the rule of descent. Here, too, the change in the rule of descent may be put down in the main to economic causes also in a broad sense. Dumping was not in those days a question of practical politics; the problem was to prevent the neighbours from pursuing the policy of the free and open port. The necessity of protecting tribal and group property in land and game would naturally tend to bind men closer and closer, in proportion as the pressure from without became greater. It is perhaps hardly accidental that the main area of male descent is that which has also developed the Intichiuma ceremonies.

If Prof. Gregory's view[1] that the occupation of Victoria by the natives dates back no more than 300 years is correct, we may perhaps see in the migration one cause of the rise of patriliny. Anything which tended to shake the influence of the mother's kin would increase the father's power; and the need of

[1] *Proc. R. S. Vict.* XVII, 120.

protecting newly established groups from the incursions of their neighbours would be more urgent than in older districts. As we have seen, the first mentioned cause has elsewhere had little direct effect; but it may well have played a larger part under the novel conditions of migration and occupation of fresh territory.

In South Queensland the fractionation of tribes seems to have gone further than elsewhere, unless we suppose that we have here an area, where, as in California, pressure from without has crowded together the remnants of many tribes. Although it is not obvious how the multiplication of distinct tribes has favoured patrilineal descent, we may, at any rate, say that the conditions in the area are exceptional; possibly it was more fruitful than the greater part of the continent; if so personal property in the shape of trees, etc., which we have already seen in existence in this area, would play a more important *rôle* here, and may well have determined the transition to patrilineal descent.

# CHAPTER III.

## DEFINITIONS AND HISTORY.

Definitions: tribe, sub-tribe, local group, phratry, class, totem kin. "Blood" and "shade." Kamilaroi type. History of Research in Australia. General sketch.

BEFORE proceeding to deal with the Australian facts it will be well to define the terminology to be employed, and give a brief survey of a typical organisation. Looking at the population from the territorial point of view in the first place, we find aggregates of tribes; these may be termed *nations.* The component tribes are friendly, one with another; they may and often do hold initiation ceremonies and other ceremonials in common; although the language is usually syntactically the same, and though they contain many words in common, the vocabularies differ to such an extent that members of different tribes are not mutually intelligible. How far the occurrence of identical kinship organisation and nomenclature should be taken as indicating a still larger unity than the nation is a difficult question. *Primâ facie* the nation is a relatively late phenomenon; but the distribution of the names of kinship organisations, as will be shown later, indicates that communication, if not alliance, existed over a wide area at some periods, which it is difficult to suppose were anything but remote.

The idea of the *tribe* has already been defined. It is a community which occupies a definite area, recognises its solidarity and possesses a common speech or dialects of the same.

Between the tribe and the family occur various subdivisions, known as sub-tribes, hordes, local groups, etc., but without any very clear definition of their nature. It appears, however, that the tribal area is sometimes so parcelled out that property in it is vested, not in the tribe as a whole, but in the *local group*, which welcomes fellow-tribesmen in times of plenty, but has the right of punishing intruders of the same tribe who seek for food without permission; for a non-tribesman the penalty is death. In some cases the local group is little more than an undivided family including three generations; it may then occupy and own an area of some ten miles radius. In other cases the term is applied to a larger aggregate, the nature and rights of which are not strictly defined; it may number some hundreds of persons and form one-third of the whole tribe; it seems best to denominate such an aggregate by the name of *sub-tribe*.

The term *family* may be retained in its ordinary sense.

Superposed on the tribal organisation are the kinship organisations, which, in the case of most Australian tribes, are independent of locality. Leaving out of account certain anomalous tribes, it may be said broadly that an Australian tribe is divided into two sets, called phratries, primary classes, moieties, etc. by various authors; the term used in the present work for these divisions is *phratry*. Membership of a phratry depends on birth and is taken *directly* from the mother (*matrilineal descent*) or father (*patrilineal descent*).

In Queensland and part of N. S. Wales the phratry is again subdivided, and four *intermarrying classes* (sometimes called sub-phratries) are formed, two of which make up each phratry. In North Australia and Queensland a further subdivision of each of these classes is found, making eight in all. Descent in the classes is *indirect* matrilineal or indirect[1] patrilineal, the child belonging to the mother's or father's phratry as before, but being assigned to the class of that phratry to which the mother or father does not belong. The classes of father and son together are called a *couple*. The parent from whom the phratry and class name are thus derived is said to be the *determinant spouse*.

These phratries and classes regulate marriage. It is forbidden to marry within one's own phratry. This custom is termed *exogamy*. When the husband removes and lives in his wife's group the marriage is *matrilocal*; if the wife removes it is *patrilocal*.

[1] Save in the Anula and Mara tribes.

In addition to the division into classes each phratry is further divided into a number of *totem kins*. A *totem* is usually a species of animals or plants; a body of human beings stands in a certain peculiar relation to the totem species and is termed the totem kin; each member of a totem kin is termed a *kinsman*. Membership of the totem kin usually descends directly from parent to child.

The existence of these kinship organisations is universally recognised. Mr R. H. Mathews has recently asserted the existence of yet another form and at the same time controverted the accepted views as to the operation and meaning of those described above. He distinguishes in certain tribes of New South Wales kinship organisations running across the phratries; these are of two kinds, according to the author, but they do not seem to differ in function. They are termed by Mr Mathews "*blood*" and "*shade*" divisions, and are held by him to be the names of the really exogamous groups. The subject is discussed in detail below.

In order to make the working of these regulations plain, let us take as an example the Kamilaroi tribe of N. S. Wales, with two phratries, four classes and various totem kins. The phratries are named Dilbi and Kupathin; Dilbi is divided into two classes, Muri and Kubi; Kupathin into Kumbo and Ipai. The Dilbi totems, which may belong to either of the classes, are kangaroo, opossum and iguana; those of Kupathin are emu, bandicoot and black snake. Every member of the tribe has his own phratry, class and totem; these all come to him by descent.

We have little or no information as to the local grouping of the Kamilaroi tribes, but it was possibly not unlike that of some of the tribes to the north-west. In the case of the latter the tribal area was some 3000 sq. miles in extent, it was split up into smaller areas, thirty or more in number, which were the property of the local groups; a local group consisted frequently of three generations of relatives. When we come to deal below with marriage regulations it will be shown that husband, wife and child under the four-class system all belong to different classes; there were therefore in each group at least three classes, if not four, and consequently members of two phratries. If we assume that the same conditions prevailed among the Kamilaroi, the local groups would then be made up of members of both the Dilbi and Kupathin phratries; and probably all four classes, Muri, Kubi, Ipai and Kumbo, would be found in each group, which in Australia varied in size according to local conditions from 20 or 30 to 200; under special conditions, such as prevailed in the neighbourhood of Lake Alexandrina, the number might run up to 600 or more, but this was exceptional.

From the fact that the totems are divided between the phratries it is clear that the local group may also have members of all the six totem kins mentioned above, among its members.

The rules by which marriage and descent are regulated are apparently very complicated but practically very simple. Taking the Kamilaroi tribe again, the rule is that Muri marries Butha (a female Kumbo) and their children are Ipai and Ipatha: Kubi marries Ipatha and their children are Kumbo and Butha; in each case the children belong to the same phratry as the mother but to the other class in that phratry. This is termed indirect matrilineal descent.

The rule of descent for the totem among the Kamilaroi was simpler; membership of a totem kin descends directly from a mother to her child. The combined effect of these rules is that if, for example, a male Dilbi of the Muri class and iguana totem wants to marry, he must choose a wife of the Kupathin phratry, the Kumbo class, and either the emu, bandicoot, or black snake totems; suppose he marries an emu woman; then his children are of the Kupathin phratry, the Ipai (or Ipatha) class, and the emu totem. These regulations are naturally more complicated among the eight-class tribes; on the other hand, where only phratries and totems are found, but no classes, descent is much simpler; for in each case the child takes the phratry and totem of its mother, where matrilineal descent prevails, or of its father, where patrilineal descent is found.

The general rule in Australia is that the wife goes to live with her husband; in other words, she leaves the local group in which she was born and becomes a member of her husband's local group. The effect of this is very different according as descent is reckoned through the mother or through the father. Taking the Kamilaroi again, the Muri-iguana man brings into his group a Butha-emu woman; their children are Ipatha-emu. If, therefore, a local group is made up of the descendants of a single family, the phratry, class, and totem names vary from generation to generation; for the girls go to other groups, and the men bring in wives of a phratry, class, and totem different, as a rule, from their own; the children of the next generation take their kinship names directly or indirectly from the mother.

If, on the other hand, descent is reckoned through the father, the phratry and totem names are always the same from generation to generation; from this it follows that the phratry of the wife, who comes from without, is also the same from generation to generation, though her totem name does not of necessity remain the same. The class name alternates both in the case of the family and of the wives in successive generations. It has already been pointed out that reckoning of descent in the male line tends to bring about local grouping of the kinship organisations. In the eight-class tribes, and in parts of Victoria, the phratries, elsewhere the totem kins, tend to be or are actually limited to certain portions of the tribal area.

Our knowledge of these matters has not, of course, been gained at a bound. Before indicating the present extent of our information, it may be well to give an historical sketch of early discoveries in this field.

Some seventy years ago the attention of students of primitive social institutions was drawn to the marriage regulations of the Indian tribes of North America by an article in *Archaeologia Americana*[1]; in which the author, drawing his conclusions partly from earlier writers, partly from his own investigations, showed that the totem kin was an exogamous group, while in some cases the kin bearing the name of a given totem were not only exogamous, but not even permitted to choose their wives from any of the other kins at will, being restricted in their choice to certain groups or, in many cases, to a single group of totem kins, according as the tribe was arranged in two or more phratries.

[1] Vol. II.

At least two observers had detected the existence of Australian organisations of the same nature as the American phratries, so far as our scanty information from West Australia goes, even before the publication of *Archaeologia Americana*. The honour of being the first to publish information on the subject belongs to Nind, who had spent some time in the neighbourhood of King George's Sound in 1829, and published his observations on native customs in the *Journal of the Royal Geographical Society*[1] for 1832. Close on his heels came the authors of *Journals of Explorations in West Australia*, which appeared in 1833, and described journeys undertaken between 1829 and 1832.

The phratries were discovered in South Australia by the Rev. C. W. Schürmann, whose Vocabulary[2], published in 1844, contains a mention of the Parnkalla phratries, without, however, any indication of their connection with marriage customs and exogamy. Five years earlier, however, Lieutenant, afterwards Sir George Grey, had observed institutions of the nature of totem kins, phratries, or intermarrying classes in West Australia, and had detected their connection with the marriage laws of the natives[3].

In 1841 and 1842, G. F. Moore[4] called attention to the grouping of the native divisions or kins, and anticipated Schürmann, as will be shown later. Grey, before the publication of his *Journal*, had read the *Archaeologia*; but though he mentions the naming of "families" after animals, he makes no mention of any grouping, but merely distinguishes between "families" and "local names." Some of the names which he gives seem to be those of phratries, and if he had been led by his study of *Archaeologia Americana* to the discovery of exogamic regulations dealing with the relations of individual totem kins to one another, it seems on the whole probable that he would not have overlooked the grouping of the kins which is, with certain exceptions, of a more or less local character, common to the whole of Australia, so far as our information goes.

[1] Vol. I, p. 38.

[2] *Vocabulary*, *s.v.* Kararu.

[3] Grey, *Journals*, II, 228.

[4] *Descriptive Vocabulary*, p. 3 etc.; *Colonial Mag.* V, 222.

Singularly enough this information, very full, relatively, for the eastern and central tribes, has, so far as South-West Australia is concerned, only just been completed, although more than sixty years have elapsed since Grey wrote, the last twenty of which have seen much additional light thrown on the organisation of the tribes of the remainder of the continent.

The American tribes, where simple totemic exogamy is not the rule, are organised in two and sometimes three or more, up to ten, phratries. It is possible that Grey, in spite of his attention having been drawn to the bi- or trichotomous organisation of American totem kins, failed to understand the Australian system owing to the presence of an element, discovered a few years later at a point remote from the scene of Grey's researches, to which no American analogue exists. In addition to the grouping of the kins into phratries, the Australian tribes over a large part of the continent subdivide each phratry into two or four classes or "castes," as they were frequently termed by the early investigators. The effect of the class system is to further limit the choice of a given individual, restricted to one-half of the women of the tribe under the simple phratry system, to one-fourth of them or one-eighth, as the case may be. Probably the first person to publish the fact of the existence of these classes, which he regarded as differing in rank, was C. P. Hodgson[1], who found them in 1846 among the blacks of Wide Bay. From a letter of Leichardt's however it appears that the discovery must have been made nearly simultaneously by several observers. Writing in 1847[2], he says that the castes are the most interesting and most obscure feature among the tribes to the northward, and mentions F. N. Isaacs as having noticed the existence of the classes among the natives of Darling Downs, adding that Capt. Macarthur had also found them among the Monobar tribes of the Coburg Peninsula. "These castes," he adds, "are probably intimately connected with the laws of intermarriage."

If Leichardt's words mean, as apparently they do, that the Monobar classes are regulative of marriage, and if his information was correct, the first mention of classes in Australia is

[1] *Australian Reminiscences*, p. 212.

[2] Bunce, 23 *Years Wanderings*, p. 116.

3—2

found, not in Hodgson's work, but in Wilson's account[1]. Neither he, however, nor Stokes[2], who mentions them as existing among the Limba Karadjee, makes any mention of their connection with marriage regulations. And Earl, at a later period, omits in like manner to say what constituted membership of a caste, though he states that they differed in rank. The names—Manjarojally (fire people), Manjarwuli (land people), and Mambulgit (makers of nets, perhaps, therefore, water people), as well as the anomalous number of the classes, seem to indicate that they are of a somewhat different nature to the real intermarrying classes found elsewhere[3]. It is of course well known that the initiation ceremonies and totemic system of the northern tribes on both sides of the Gulf of Carpentaria differ somewhat widely from the normal Australian form.

None of the observers hitherto mentioned can be said however to have applied himself to the scientific study of the questions raised by the facts which they recorded. Anthropology was in those days in its infancy. The first to make a really serious effort to clear up the many difficult questions, some of them still matters of controversy, which a closer study of the native marriage customs brought to the surface, was a missionary anthropologist, a class of which England has produced all too few. In 1853 the Rev. William Ridley published the first of many studies of the Kamilaroi speaking tribes, and, thanks to the impetus given to the investigation of systems of relationship and allied questions by Lewis Morgan, was the pioneer of a series of efforts which have rescued for us at the nick of time a record of the social organisation of many tribes which under European influence are now rapidly losing or have already lost all traces of their primitive customs, if indeed they have not, like the tribes formerly resident at Adelaide and other centres of population, been absolutely exterminated by contact with the white man with his vices and his civilisation, or by the less gentle method euphemis-

[1] *J.R.G.S.* IV, 171, p. 88, *Narrative of a Voyage round the World* p. 88.

[2] *Discoveries* (1846), I, 393; cf. *Kamilaroi and Kurnai*, p. 64.

[3] Cf. the local groups of the Yuin, the Wiradjeri and other tribes, Howitt, *passim*.

tically termed "dispersion," which, if other nations were the offenders, we should term massacre.

After Mr Ridley, Messrs Fison and Howitt turned their attention to the Kamilaroi group of tribes. The progress of these investigations is traced, historically and controversially, in the second series of Maclennan's *Studies in Ancient History*, and it is unnecessary to deal with it in detail. More and more light was thrown on totemism, marriage regulations, and intermarrying classes by the persistent efforts of Mr Howitt, by Dr Frazer's little work on Totemism, and by other students, until it seemed that the main features of Australian social organisation had been clearly established, when in 1898 the researches of Messrs Spencer and Gillen seemed to do much to overthrow all recognised principles, so far as the totemic regulation of marriage was concerned. How far this is actually the case it is unnecessary to consider here. It may be said however that the work of these two investigators and the enquiries of Dr Roth in North Queensland make it more than ever a matter for regret that the British Empire, the greatest colonial power that the world has ever seen, will not afford the few thousand pounds needed to put such researches on a firm basis.

Having defined the various terms, and shown the actual working of the system by the aid of the best known example, we may now pass, after this brief historical sketch of the development of our knowledge, to the task of giving the broad outlines of the phratry and class organisations.

If our knowledge of Australian phratries and classes is far from exhaustive, we have at any rate a fair knowledge of the distribution of the various types whose existence is generally recognised; that is to say, we can delimit the greater part of the continent according to whether the tribes show two phratries only, or two phratries, which may be anonymous, with the further subdivision into four classes, or into eight classes. We also know approximately the limits of the matrilineal and patrilineal systems. New South Wales, Victoria, the southern portion of Queensland and Northern Territory, the eastern part of South Australia, and the coastal regions of West Australia, are now known with more or less accuracy from the point of view of kinship organisations. On the other hand, from the Cape York Peninsula, and the part of Northern Territory north of Lat. 15°, we have little if any information. The south coast and its hinterland from 135° westwards, as far as King George's Sound, is virtually a terra incognita; in fact beyond the south-western corner and the fringe which lies along the coast we know little of the West Australian blacks, and the frontiers between the various systems must in these areas be regarded as purely provisional.

Broadly speaking, the tribes of the whole of the known area of Australia, certain coast regions of comparatively small extent excepted, have a dichotomous kinship organisation. The accompanying map (Map II) shows how the various forms are distributed. Along most of the south coast, and up a belt broken perhaps in the northern portion, running through the centre of the continent in Lat. 137°, are found two phratries without intermarrying classes; for the area west of Lat. 130° we have, it is true, only one datum, which gives no information as to the area to which it applies; this portion of the field therefore is assigned only provisionally to the two-phratry system. On the Bloomfield River, which runs into Weary Bay, associated with the name of Captain Cook, is an isolated two-phratry organisation, unless indeed we may assume that the class names have either been overlooked or have passed out of use.

The four-class system extends over the greater part of New South Wales, and Queensland; a narrow belt runs through the north of South Australia and broadens till it embraces the whole coastline of West Australia, the north-eastern area excluded. An isolated four-class system, which does not regulate marriage, is found in the Yorke Peninsula of South Australia.

The eight-class system forms a compact mass, between the Gulf of Carpentaria and Roebuck Bay, extending south as far as Lat. 25° in the centre of Australia.

In reality the rule of the eight-class system extends considerably further south, but the classes are nameless or altogether non-existent. Thus, the southern Arunta have nominally four classes, but each of these has two sections, so that the final result is as though they were an eight-class tribe. In the same way the marriage regulations of the two-phratry Dieri are such that choice is limited among them precisely as it would be if they had eight classes. The same may be true of the remainder of the western branch of the four-class system, which is closely allied in name to the Arunta type; the boundary between the related sets of names is unknown.

Among the Narrinyeri and the Yuin the kinship organisation, which is confined to totemic groups, takes a local form; here the regulation of marriage depends on considerations of the residence of the pair. Local exogamy also prevails among the unorganised Kurnai. The Chepara appear to have had no organisation, and among the Narrangga ties of consanguinity constituted the sole bar to marriage. We are not however concerned with the problems presented by these aberrant types of organisation, to which no further reference is made in the present work.

The area covered by the dichotomous organisations is divided almost equally between matrilineal and patrilineal tribes. The latter occupy the region north of Lat. 30° and west of an irregular line running from Long. 137° to 140° or thereabouts. In addition a portion of Victoria and the region west of Brisbane form isolated patrilineal groups. The problem presented by these anomalous areas has already been discussed in the chapter on the Rule of Descent. Where local exogamy is the rule, kinship is also virtually patrilineal.

In the remainder of Australia, non-organised tribes of course excepted, the rule of descent is matrilineal, save that in North Queensland a small tribe on the Annan River prefers paternal descent. The accompanying map shows the distribution of the two forms.

RULE OF DESCENT.

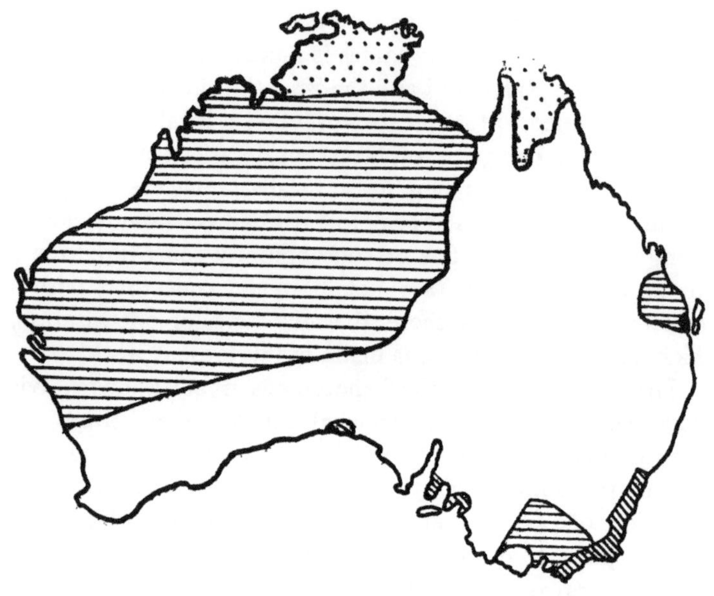

MAP I.

White — Matrilineal descent, phratry or class.

(horizontal lines) — Patrilineal descent, phratry or class.

(diagonal lines) — Patrilineal descent, phratry or class of totem.

Black — No kinship organisation.

(dots) — Unknown.

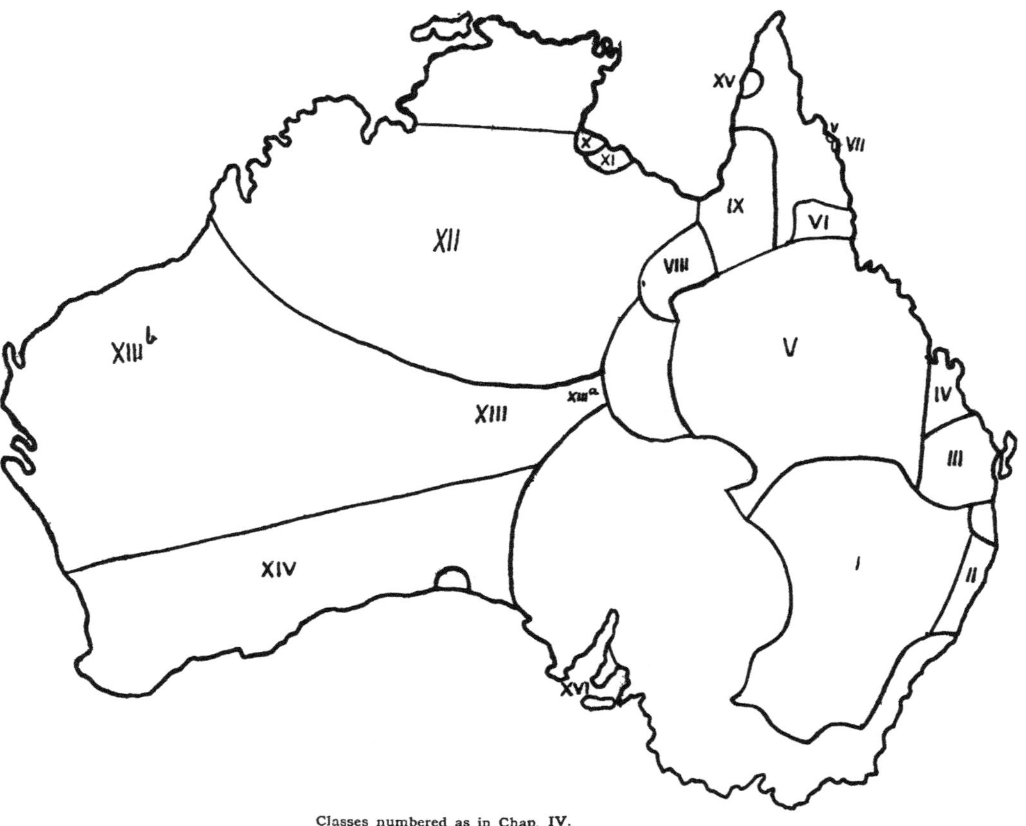


Classes numbered as in Chap. IV.

For anomalous and non-class areas see Map I.

PHRATRY ORGANISATIONS. MAP III.

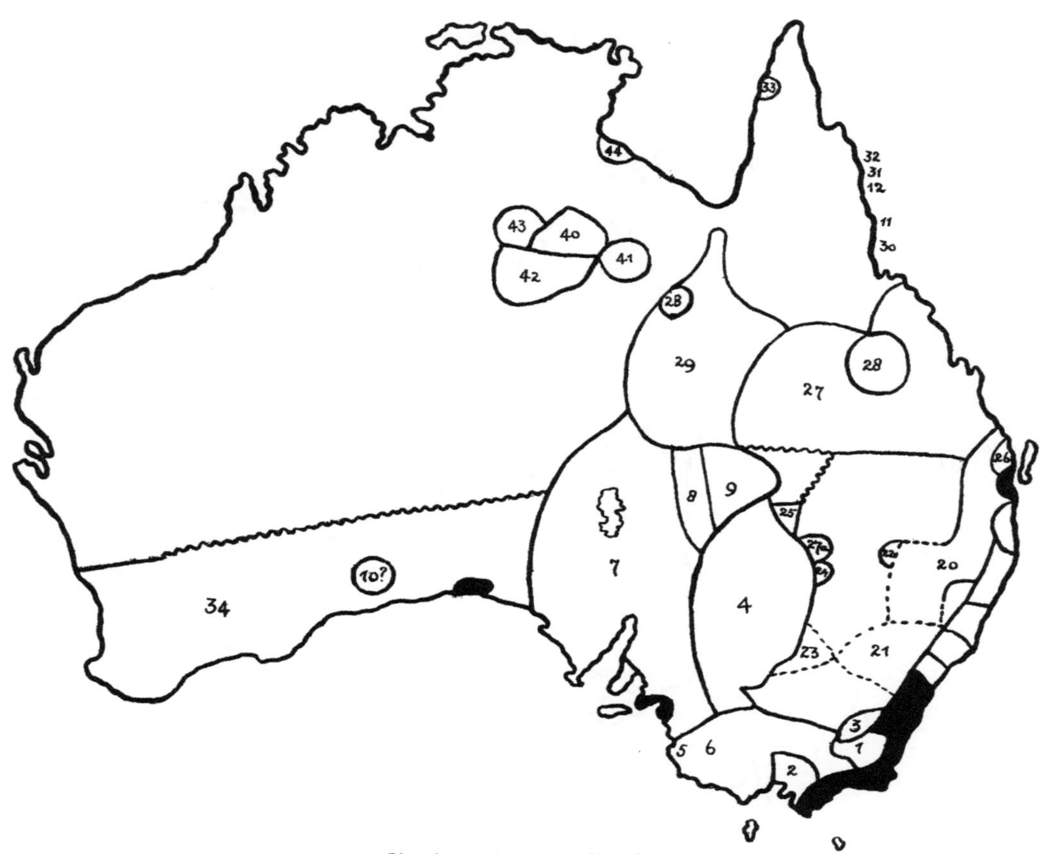


Phratries numbered as in Chap. IV.
Black areas—no phratries.

# CHAPTER IV.

## TABLES OF CLASSES, PHRATRIES, ETC.

IN order to facilitate reference and to diminish the necessity for footnotes a survey of classes and phratries is here given. It will be well to explain how they are arranged.

In the two-phratry system the rule of intermarriage is clear; a man of phratry $A$ marries a woman of phratry $B$ and *vice versa.* The direct descent of the kinship name is obviously the rule.

The four classes are arranged according to the phratries; the normal rule is that a man $A1$ marries $B1$, $A2$ marries $B2$; their children are in matrilineal tribes $A2$ and $B2$, in patrilineal $B2$ and $A2$. In the patrilineal Mara and Anula, by exception, the rule of descent is direct; it will be remembered that a dichotomy of the classes prevails, so that they really belong to the eight-class system.

In the eight-class system and among the nominally four-class southern Arunta the intermarriage and descent is as follows, according to Spencer and Gillen;

$$\frac{A1}{B1} = A4, \qquad \frac{B1}{A1} = B3,$$

$$\frac{A2}{B2} = A3, \qquad \frac{B2}{A2} = B4,$$

$$\frac{A3}{B3} = A2, \qquad \frac{B3}{A3} = B1,$$

$$\frac{A4}{B4} = B4, \qquad \frac{B4}{A4} = B2.$$

In each case the male is the numerator, the woman the denominator, and the = shows the child.

Tribes with conterminous territories usually know what phratries and classes are equivalent in their systems. In the tables which follow the phratries and the classes of matrilineal tribes are arranged to show this correspondence so far as it is known. A * shows that no information on the point is to hand. A rearrangement of patrilineal classes is necessary to make them equivalent to the organisations of matrilineal tribes; this cannot be shown in the tables; but full details will be found in the works of Spencer and Gillen. A † indicates patrilineal descent.

Where the names of phratries and classes are translated, the meanings are shown in the tables; where the authorities do not give the translation but a word of the same form is in use in the tribe or group of tribes the meanings are given in round brackets; words in use in neighbouring tribes are put in square brackets.

## TABLE I.

### *The Class Names.*

| | *Class names* | *Feminine* | *Meaning* |
|---|---|---|---|
| I. | Muri (Bya)[1] | Matha | (Red kangaroo) |
| | Kubi | Kubitha | (Opossum) |
| | Kumbo (Wōmbee)[2] | Butha | |
| | Ipai | Ipatha | (Eaglehawk) |

These class names are found in the following tribes:

Kamilaroi (Howitt, p. 107); Wiradjeri (*ib.* 107); Wonghi (*ib.* 108); Euahlayi (Mrs L. Parker, *Euahlayi Tribe*, p. 13); Ngeumba (Mathews in *Eth. Notes*, p. 5); Murawari (*id.* in *Proc. R. G. S. Qu.*, 1906, 55); Moree (*R. G. S. Qu.* x, 20); Turribul (*R. S. Vict.* I, 102); Wollaroi (Howitt, 109); on Narran R. (Curr, I, 117); Pikumbul (*ib.*); Unghi (Howitt, 217); Peechera (Curr, III, 271); Wailwun (*ib.* I, 116); Wonnaruah (*Sci. Man*, I, 180); Geawegal (Howitt, 266).

Associated with these class names are the following phratry names:

| | | | |
|---|---|---|---|
| (*a*) | Kamilaroi, etc. | Dilbi | Kupathin |
| (*b*) | Wiradjeri to N. of Lachlan | Budthurung | Mukula |
| (*c*) | Wonghibon | Ngielbumurra | Mukumurra (Howitt) |
| (*d*) | " & Ngeumba | Ngumbun / Numbun | Ngurrawan (Mathews) |
| (*e*) | Euahlayi | Gwaigullean | Gwaimudthen |
| (*f*) | Murawari | Girrana | Merugulli |

[1] The Darkinung have Bya for Muri (*J. R. S. N. S. W.* XXXI, 170).

[2] Some of the Wiradjeri have Wōmbee for Kumbo (Gribble, 113).

| | *Class names* | *Feminine* |
|---|---|---|
| II. | Kurbo | Kooran |
| | Marro | Kurgan |
| | Wombo | Wirrikin |
| | Wirro | Wongan |

The proper arrangement of these names is unknown.

*Tribe:* Kombinegherry (*J. A. I.* XIII, 304; Howitt, 105).

*Science of Man* (IV, 8) gives:

| | |
|---|---|
| Carribo | Gooroona |
| Maroongah | Carrigan |
| Womboongah | Werrican |
| Weiro | Warganbah |

For the Anaywan, Thangatty, etc., R. H. Mathews gives (*J. R. S. N. S. W.* XXXI, 169):

| | |
|---|---|
| Irpoong | Matyang |
| Marroong | Arrakan |
| Imboong | Irrakadena |
| Irroong | Palyang |

| | *Class name* (*Fem. termination, -an or -gan*) | *Meaning* |
|---|---|---|
| III†[1]. | Parang (Moroon) | (Black wallaby. Emu) |
| | Bunda | [Kangaroo] |
| | Balgoin (Banjoor, Pandur) | (Red wallaby. Native bear) |
| | Theirwain | (Kangaroo) |

*Tribes:* Maryborough tribes (Howitt, 117); Kabi (Curr, III, 163): Kiabara (*J. A. I.* XIII, 305); ? (Hodgson, 212; Mathew, *Eaglehawk*, 100); Wide Bay (Curr, I, 117).

For the Emon, Howitt (p. 109) gives:

Barah
Bondan
Bondurr
Taran

With these classes are associated the phratries:

| | | | |
|---|---|---|---|
| (*a*) | The Maryborough tribes and the Kiabara | Dilbi | Kupathin. |
| (*b*) | Dippil | Deeajee | Karpeun |

are the forms given by Mathews (*Proc. Am. Phil. Soc.* XXXVIII, 329).

[1] Male descent.

| | Class names (Fem. termination, -an) | Meaning |
|---|---|---|
| IV. | Karilbura | Barrimundi |
| | Munal | Hawk |
| | Kurpal | Good water |
| | Kuialla (Koodala) | Iguana |

*Tribes:* Kuinmurbura (*J. A. I.* XIII, 341; Howitt, 111). The Taroombul have the form Koodala (*Proc. R. S. Qu.* XIII, 41).

For the Kangulu, Mathews (*J. R. S. N. S. W.* XXXIII, 111) gives:

Banniar[1]
Banjoor
Koorpal
Kearra

With these may be compared Howitt's (p. 111):

Kairawa
Bunjur
Bunya
Jarbain (? Tarbain)

The phratries associated with these are:

| | Tribe | | |
|---|---|---|---|
| (a) | Kuinmurbura | Witteru | Yungaru |
| (b) | Kangulu | Wutthuru | Yungnuru |

| | Class names | Fem. termination | Meaning |
|---|---|---|---|
| V. | Wongo | | |
| | Kubaru (Ubur, Obu) | -an | (Gidea tree) |
| | Bunburi (Anbeir, Unburri, Bunbai) | | |
| | Koorgilla (Urgilla) | | |

*Tribes:* Ungorri (Howitt, 109); Kogai (Curr, I, 117; *J. A. I.* XIII, 337); Yuipera etc. (Curr, III, 45, 64; *J. A. I.* XIII, 302); Akulbura, Bathalibura (Howitt, 113, 141); Wakelbura (Howitt, 112); on Belyando (Curr, III, 26); Dalebura (Howitt, 113), Buntamurra (Howitt, 113, 226); Purgoma (Roth, 66); Jouon (*ib.* 67); Pitta-Pitta, Goa, Miorli (Roth, 56–7); Ringa-Ringa (*J. A. I.* XIII, 337); Mittakoodi (Roth, 56–7); Woonamurra (*ib.*); Yerunthully (Mathews in *R. G. S. Qu.* X, 30); Badieri (*id. ib.* 1905, 55).

[1] Some of the names given by Howitt and Mathews seem to be identical with those of the Kiabara, but there is a difficulty about the arrangement, for Koorpal-Keeara = Yungnuru = Bunya-Jarbain; but Banniar, which seems to be the same as Bunya, falls in the other moiety.

With these class names are associated the phratries

| | | | |
|---|---|---|---|
| (*a*) | Kogai, Wakelbura etc. | Wuthera | Mallera |
| (*b*) | Yuipera, Bathalibura | Wootaroo | Yungaroo |
| (*c*) | Purgoma | Naka | Tunna |
| (*d*) | Jouon | Chepa | Junna |
| (*e*) | Pitta-Pitta etc., Mitta-koodi, Woonamura | Ootaroo | Pakoota |
| (*f*) | Badieri | Wootaroo | Yungo |

Aberrant forms, probably inaccurate, are given by Curr (II, 424) for Halifax Bay: Korkoro, Korkeen, Wongo, Wotero; by Lumholtz (p. 199) for the Herbert R.: Gorilla, Gorgero, Gorgorilla, Otero, by Curr (II, 468) for the Yukkaburra: Utheroo, Multheroo, Yungaroo, Goorgilla.

On the Tully R. Roth (*Ethn. Bull.* V, 20) found the following:

| | *Class names* |
|---|---|
| VI. | Karavangi |
| | Chikun |
| | Kurongon |
| | Kurkilla |

With these may be compared the names given by Mathews for the Warkeman (*J. R. S. N. S. W.* XXXII, 109, 251):

Karpungie
Cheekungie
Kellungie
Koopungie

On the Annan R. we find (Howitt, 118) with male descent:

| | *Class names* | *Meaning* |
|---|---|---|
| VII. | Wandi | Eaglehawk |
| | Walar | Bee |
| | Jorro | Bee |
| | Kutchal | Saltwater Eaglehawk |

With these are associated the phratries:

| | | |
|---|---|---|
| (*a*) | Walar | Murla |

| | |
|---|---|
| VIII. | Ranya (Arenia) |
| | Rara (Arara) |
| | Loora |
| | Awunga (Arawongo) |

*Tribes:* Wollongurma (Roth, 68); Goothanto (Mathews in *J. R. S. N.S. W.* XXXIII, 109).

Connected with these forms are:

*Class names*

Barry (Ahjereena)
Ararey (Arrenynung)
Jury [? Loory] (Perrynung)
Mungilly (Mahngal) [diamond snake][1]

*Tribes*: Koogobathy (*J. A. I.* XIII, 303); Koonjan etc. (Mathews in *J. R. S. N. S. W.* XXXIII, 110, XXXIV, 135). Probably Perrynung and Ahjereenya should be transposed.

| | *Class names* | *Feminine* |
|---|---|---|
| IX. | Jimmilingo | Carburungo |
| | Badingo | Ngarrangungo |
| | Maringo[2] | Munjungo |
| | Youingo (Kapoodungo) | Goothamungo |

*Tribes:* Miappe (Roth, 56–7); Mycoolon (*J. A. I.* XIII, 302); Workoboongo (Roth, *ib.*).

For the Kalkadoon, Roth (*ib.*) gives:

Kunggilungo
Patingo
Toonbeungo
Marinungo[2]

With these are associated the phratries:

| | | | |
|---|---|---|---|
| (*a*) | Kalkadoon | Ootaroo | Mullara |
| (*b*) | Miappe | Woodaroo | Pakutta |

*Class names*

X. Murungun
Mumbali
Purdal
Kuial

*Tribe:* Mara (*Northern Tribes*, 119).

With these the phratry names:

(*a*) Urku Ua

In this tribe is male descent, and, as in the S. Arunta, the classes are themselves divided; for equivalence the numbers of the eight-class system are arranged (*Nor. Tr.* 123), 1, 4; 3, 2; 5, 7; 6, 8.

[1] Curr, II, 478.

[2] Marinungo seems to be the same as Maringo but is not equivalent.

## TABLE Ia: XII. CLASS NAMES OF EIGHT-CLASS TRIBES.

| Oolawunga[1] etc. | Bingongina[2] | Umbaia[3] | Yookala[4] etc. | Binbinga[5] | Gnanji[6] | Worgaia[7] | Yangarel |
|---|---|---|---|---|---|---|---|
| Janna<br>*Nanakoo* | Thama } Tchana }<br>*Nana* | Tjinum<br>*Ninum* | Jinagoo | Tjuanaku<br>*Niriuma* | Uanuku<br>*Nuanakurna* | Wairgu | Narrabala<br>*Neonam* |
| Jimidya<br>*Namaja* | Tjimita<br>*Namita* | Tjulum<br>*Nulum* | Joolanjegoo | Tjulantjuka<br>*Nurlum* | Tjulantjuka<br>*Nurlanjukurna* | Blaingunjhu | Bolangie<br>*Nolangn* |
| Dhalyeree | Thalirri<br>*Nalirri* | Paliarinji<br>*Paliarina* | Bullaranjee | Paliarinji<br>*Paliarina* | Paliarinja<br>*Paliarina* | Biliarinthu | Bulleringie<br>*Nulyar* |
| Dhongaree | Thungarie<br>*Nungari* | Pungarinji<br>*Pungarinia* | Bungaranjee | Pungarinji<br>*Pungarina* | Pungarinji<br>*Pungarinia* | Pungarinju | Bongaring<br>*Nongar* |
| Joolama<br>*Nowala* | Tjurla<br>*Nala* | Tjurulum<br>*Nurulum* | Jooralagoo | Tjurulum<br>*Nurulum* | Uralaku<br>*Nuralakurna* | Warrithu | Burralangi<br>*Nurral* |
| Jungalla | Thungalla<br>*Nungalla* | Thungallum<br>*Nungallum* | Jungalagoo | Thungallum<br>*Nungallum* | Thungallaku<br>*Nungallakurna* | Kingelunju | Kunuller<br>*Nungal* |
| Jeemara | Tjimara<br>*Nunalla* | Tjamerum<br>*Niameragun* | Jameragoo | Tjamerum<br>*Niamerum* | Tjameraku<br>*Niamaku* | Tjameramu | Kommera<br>*Nemura* |
| Jambijana<br>*Nambean* | Tjambitjina<br>*Nambitjina* | Yakomari<br>*Yakomarin* | Yukamurra | Yakomari<br>*Yakomarina* | Yakomari<br>*Yakomarina* | Ikamaru | Yakomari<br>*Jumeyu* |

[1] Mathews in *Proc. R. G. S. Qu.*, X, 72.

[2] *Northern Tribes*, 101.

[3] *Ib.*, 100, cf. *J. R. S. N. S. W.*, XXXIV, 121; XXXIX, 105.

[4] Mathews in *Proc. Am. Phil. Soc.*, XXXVIII, 77.

[5] *Northern Tribes*, 111.

[6] *Northern Tribes*, 101.

[7] *Northern Tribes*, 101.

[8] Mathews in *J. R. S. N. S. W*

[9] Mathews in *J. R. S. N. S. W*

[10] Mathews in *J. R. S. N. S.*

[11] *Northern Tribes*, 100; cf. XVI, 72, 73.

| lachie[9] | Yungmunnie[10] | Tjingillie[11] | Ilpirra[12] / Arunta / Kaitish / Iliaura | Warramunga[13] / Walpari / Wulmala | Meening[14] | Mayoo[15] | Koorangie[16] etc. |
|---|---|---|---|---|---|---|---|
| balangie<br>ie | Unwannee<br>*Imbannee* | Thamininja<br>*Namininja* | Panunga | Thapanunga<br>*Napanunga* | Chowan<br>*Nowana* | Chinuma<br>*Nanagoo* | Janna<br>*Nanakoo* |
| gie | Eemitch<br>*Immadena* | Tjimininja<br>*Truminginja* | Uknaria | Tjinguri<br>*Namigili* | Choongoora<br>*Nangili* | Choongoora<br>*Narbeeta* | Jamada |
| ingie | Uwallaree<br>*Imballaree* | Thalaringinja<br>*Nalaringinja* | Bulthara<br>Kabidgi<br>*Appitchana* | Tjapeltjeri<br>*Naltjeri* | Chavalya<br>*Nanajerry* | Chavalya<br>*Nabajerry* | Dhalyeree |
| ingie | Uwungaree<br>*Imbongaree* | Thungaringinta<br>*Namaringinta* | Appungerta | Thapungarti<br>*Napungerta* | Chowarding<br>*Nabungati* | Changary<br>*Nhermana* | Dhungaree |
| angie<br>hie | Urwalla<br>*Imbawalla* | Tjurulinginja<br>*Nalinginja* | Purula | Tjupila<br>*Naralu* | Chooara<br>*Nooara* | Choolima<br>*Naola* | Joolam |
| la | Yungalla<br>*Inkagalla* | Thungallininja<br>*Nalangininja* | Ungalla | Thungalla<br>*Nungalla* | Changally<br>*Nangally* | Chungalla<br>*Nungalla* | Jungalla |
| erangie<br>ngoona | Unmarra<br>*Inganmarra* | Thamaringinja<br>*Namaringinja* | Kumara | Thakomara<br>*Nakomara* | Chagarra<br>*Nagarra* | Chapota<br>*Nemira* | Jameram |
| aroo<br>nermill | Tabachin<br>*Tabadenna* | Tjapatjinginja<br>*Nambitjinginja* | Umbitchana | Tjambin<br>*Nambin* | Chambeen<br>*Nambeen* | Chambijana<br>*Nambjana* | Jummiunga |

II, 495; *Proc. R. G. S. Qu.*,

[12] *Native Tribes*, 90; cf. *Proc. R. S. Vict.*, N. S. x, 19; *T. R. S. S. A.*, xiv, 224; *J. R. S. N. S. W.*, xxxii, 72.

[13] *Northern Tribes*, 100; cf. *J. A. I.* xviii, 44; *J. R. S. N. S. W.*, xxxii, 73.

[14] Mathews in *J. R. S. N. S. W.*, xxxiii, 112; xxxv, 217.

[15] Mathews in *Proc. R. G. S. Qu.*, xvi, 70.

[16] Mathews in *Am. Phil. Soc.*, xxxviii, 78.

Leichardt (*Journal*, 447) reports from the Roper R., Gnangball, Odall, Nurumball, which from their form seem to be class names and identifiable with some of the Mara names.

*Class names*

XI. Awukaria
Roumburia
Urtalia
Wialia

*Tribe:* Anula (*Nor. Tr.* 119).

XII. For the eight-class system see Table Ia, in which it is assumed that patrilineal descent prevails in all the tribes.

With these are associated the following phratries:

| | | | |
|---|---|---|---|
| (*a*) | Umbaia, Gnanji | Illitchi | Liaritchi |
| (*b*) | Warramunga, Walpari, Wulmala | Uluuru | Kingilli |
| (*c*) | Worgaia | „ | Biingaru |
| (*d*) | Bingongina | Wiliuku | Liaraku |

Spencer and Gillen, *Nor. Tr.* pp. 100—102, 119. On p. 102 is a statement about the Bingongina inconsistent with that on the following page; according to the former the phratry names are Illitchi, Liaritchi, as among the Umbaia.

*Class names*

XIII. Panunga
Bulthara
Purula
Kumara

*Tribe:* S. Arunta (*Nat. Tr.* 90).

XIII*a*. Deringara
Gubilla
Koomara
Belthara

*Tribe*: Yoolanlanya etc. (*R. G. S. Qu.* XVI, 75).

The arrangement suggests that matrilineal descent prevails, but there is probably some error.

*Class names*

XIII*b*. Burong (Parungo)
Ballieri (Parajerri; Butcharrie)
Banaka (Boogarloo)
Kymerra (Kaiamba)

*Tribes:* Gnamo, Gnalluma (*Int. Arch.* XVI, 12); Nickol Bay and Kimberley have the alternative forms of 1, 2, and 4 (Curr, I, 296; *Kamilaroi*, 36, Mathews in *J. R. S. N. S. W.* XXXV, 220), Weedokarry (*id.* in *Proc. Am. Phil. Soc.* XXXIX, 89) have third form of 2; at Murchison R. Boorgarloo comes into use (*West Australian*, Ap. 7, 1906).

| | *Class names* | *Meaning* |
|---|---|---|
| XIV. | Tondarup (Namyungo) | Fish hawk |
| | Didaruk | Sea |
| | Ballaruk (Yangor) | (Opossum) |
| | Naganok | (Fish) |

*Tribes:* S. W. Australia, Tarderick etc. (*West. Aust.*, *loc. cit.*; Moore, *Desc. Voc.*, *Col. Mag.* V, 422.

The phratries are

| | | |
|---|---|---|
| (*a*) | Wartungmat | Munichmat |

The equivalence is unknown.

| | *Class names* |
|---|---|
| XV. | Langenam |
| | Namegor |
| | Packwicky |
| | Pamarung |

*Tribe:* Joongoongie of N. Queensland (Mathews in *Proc. Am. Phil. Soc.* XXXIX, 93).

Associated with them the phratries:

| | | |
|---|---|---|
| (*a*) | Jamagunda | Gamanutta |

The equivalence is unknown.

| | *Class names* | *Meaning* |
|---|---|---|
| XVI. | Kari | Emu |
| | Waui | Red kangaroo |
| | Wiltu | Eaglehawk |
| | Wilthuthu | Shark |

*Tribe:* Narrangga of Yorke Peninsula (Howitt, p. 130).

## TABLE II.

### *Phratry Names.*

| | *Phratries* | *Meanings* | *Name of Tribe* |
|---|---|---|---|
| 1. | †Waa(ng) | Crow | Wurunjerri[1] |
| | Bunjil or Wrepil | Eaglehawk | |
| 2. | Yuckembruk | ,, | Ngarrego[2] |
| | Merung | | |

[1] Howitt, p. 126. [2] *Id.* p. 101.

| | *Phratries* | *Meanings* | *Name of Tribe* |
|---|---|---|---|
| 3. | Umbe<br>Malian or Multa | Crow<br>Eaglehawk | Wolgal[1] etc. |
| 4. | Muquara<br>Kilpara | " | Berriait[2], Tatathi[3], Wathi-Wathi[3], Keramin[4], Waimbio[5], Barkinji[6], Milpulko[7], Wilya[7], Itchumundi[8] |
| 5. | Kumit (Gamutch, Kaputch, Kulitch) | Black cockatoo | |
| | Kroki (Krokitch, Krokage) | White cockatoo | Booandik[9], Wotjoballuk[10], Gournditchmara[11] etc. |

The feminine terminations are -egor, -gurk or -jarr.

For South-West Victoria Dawson (*Aborigines*, p. 26) gives two groups and an odd totem kin (?):

| | *Phratries* | *Meaning* | *Name of Tribe* |
|---|---|---|---|
| 6. | Kuurokeetch | Longbilled cockatoo | |
| | Kartpoerappa | Pelican | |
| | Kappatch | Banksia cockatoo | |
| | Kirtuuk | Boa snake | |
| | Kuunamit | Quail | |
| 7. | Kararu (Kiraru, Kararawa)<br>Matteri | | Dieri[12], Parnkalla & Nauo[13], Yandairunga[14], Urabunna[15] |
| 8. | Tinewa | | Yandrawontha, Yowerawarika[16] |
| | Koolpuru | (? Emu) | |
| 9. | Yungo | (? Kangaroo) | |
| | Mattera | | Kurnandaburi[17] |
| 10. | Kookoojeeba<br>Koocheebinga | | Geebera[18] |

The equivalence is not known.

| | | | |
|---|---|---|---|
| 11. | Koorabunna<br>Kooragula | | Goonganji[19] |

[1] *Id.* p. 102, Lang, *Secret*, p. 163. [2] Curr, II, 165. [3] *J. A. I.* XIII, 338; Howitt, p. 195. [4] *J. A. I.* XIV, 349. [5] Taplin, p. 17; Howitt, p. 100. [6] *J. A. I.* XIV, 348; Curr, II, 188, 195. [7] Howitt, p. 98. [8] *Id.* p. 106 n. For the Kurnai, Bunjil and Ngarregal were perhaps phratry names (Howitt, p. 135). [9] Curr, III, 461; Howitt, p. 123. [10] *Id.* p. 121. [11] *Id.* p. 124. [12] Howitt, p. 91. [13] Woods, p. 222. [14] Howitt, p. 187. [15] *Nor. Tr.* p. 60. [16] Howitt, p. 97. [17] Howitt, p. 92; Mathews in *J. R. S. N. S. W.* XXXIII, 108.

[18] Mathews in *Proc. Am. Phil. Soc.* XXXIX, 187.

[19] *Sci. Man*, I. 84; Mathews in *Proc. Am. Phil. Soc.* XXXIX, 89; in *J. R. S. N. S. W.* he reports a third name in certain districts—Koorameenya.

| | *Phratry* | | |
|---|---|---|---|
| 12. | Darboo* | | Bloomfield River[1] |
| | Tooar | | |

* The equivalence is unknown.

| | *Phratry names.* | | *Four-class system* | *Meaning* |
|---|---|---|---|---|
| 20. | Dilbi | Kupathin | Ia, IIIa† | |
| 21. | Budthurung(1) | Mukula | Ib | (1)=black duck |
| 22. | Gwaigullean | Gwaimudthen | Ie | Light blood; dark blood |
| 23. | Ngielbumurra | Mukumurra | Ic | |
| 24. | Ngumbun | Ngurrawan | Id | |
| 25. | Girana | Merugulli | If | |
| 26. | Deeajee | Karpeun | IIIb | |
| 27. | Witteru | Yungaru | IVa, b; Vb | (? Kangaroo; ? emu) |
| 27*a*. | " | Yungo | Vf | |
| 28. | " | Mallera | Va, IXa | |
| 29. | " | Pakoota | Ve, IXb | |
| 30. | Naka | Tunna | Vc | |
| 31. | Walar | Murla* | VIIa | Bee; bee |
| 32. | Cheepa | Junna | Vd | |
| 33. | Jamagunda | Gamanutta* | XIa | |
| 34. | Wartungmat | Munichmat* | XIVa | Crow; white cockatoo |
| | | | *Eight-class system* † | |
| 40. | Illitchi | Liaritchi | XIIa | |
| 41. | Uluuru | Biingaru | XIIc | (? Curlew) |
| 42. | " | Kingilli | XIIb | (? Curlew) |
| 43. | Wiliuku | Liaraku | XIId | |
| 44. | Urku | Ua | Xa | |

## TABLE III.

Allusion has been made in Chapter III to kinship organisations denominated "bloods" and "shades" by Mr R. H. Mathews. Whether it is that some observers have mistaken these for phratries or *vice versâ*, it seems that the names of the two classes of organisation are at present inextricably intermingled, as the following table shows:

| *Tribe* | *Phratry* | *Blood* | *Meaning* |
|---|---|---|---|
| Itchmundi[2] | Kilpara-Muquara | Mukulo-Ngielpuru | †Sluggish and |
| " | | Muggula-Ngipuru† | swift blood |
| Wiradjeri[3] | Mukula-Budthurung | | |
| Wonghibon[4] | Mukumura-Ngielbumura | | |

[1] Mathews in *Proc. Am. Phil. Soc.* XXXIX, 89.

[2] Howitt, p. 106 n.; Mathews in *J. R. S. N. S. W.* XXXIX, 118.

[3] *Id.* p. 107.

[4] *Id.* p. 108.

| *Tribe* | *Phratry* | *Blood* | *Meaning* |
|---|---|---|---|
| Wonghi-bon and Ngeumba[1] | Ngumbun-Ngur-rawan | Gwaigullimba-Gwaimudhan‡ | ‡Swift and sluggish blood |
| Euahlayi[2] | Gwaigullean-Gwai-mudthen | | Light and dark blooded |
| Murawari[3] | Girrana-Merugulli | Muggulu-Bumbirra§ | §Sluggish and swift blood |

## TABLE IV.

The areas covered by the different class and phratry names are not co-extensive, that is to say a class is associated with more than one phratry and *vice versâ*. The Undekerebina[4] and Yelyuyendi[5] have phratries (No. 29) which are usually associated with classes but in their case none have been noted. On the other hand it is not uncommon to find classes without the corresponding phratry names; this is the case in the eight class area, among the tribes of N. S. Wales, S. Queensland, etc.; but no special significance attaches to it unless we are certain that it is not the negligence of the observer nor the disuse of the names which has produced this state of things. On the other hand the relation of phratry and class areas is of the highest importance, as is shown in Chapter V. The following table shows the anomalies:

| *Tribe* | *Phratry* | *Class* |
|---|---|---|
| Wiradjeri | 21 | I |
| Euahlayi | 22 | I |
| Ngeumba, Wonghi | 23, or 24 | I |
| Murawari | 25 | I |
| Kiabara, etc. | 20 | III |
| Dippil | 26 | III |
| Kuinmurbura, Kongulu | 27 | IV |
| Yuipera, Badieri, Yambeena, etc. | 27 | V |
| Kogai, Wakelbura, etc. | 28 | V |
| Woonamura, Mittakoodi, Miorli, etc. | 29 | V |
| Purgoma | 30 | V |
| Jouon | 32 | V |
| Miappe | 29 | VIII |
| Kalkadoon | 28 | VIII |

[1] Mathews in *J. R. S. N. S. W.* XXXIX, 116, *Eth. Notes*, p. 5.

[2] Mrs Langloh Parker, *Euahlayi Tribe*, p. 11.

[3] Mathews in *Proc. R. G. S. Qu.*, 1905, 52.

[4] Rota, p. 56.

[5] Howitt, p. 192.

# CHAPTER V.

## PHRATRY NAMES.

The Phratriac Areas. Borrowing of Names. Their Meanings. Antiquity of Phratry Names. Eaglehawk Myths. Racial Conflicts. Intercommunication. Tribal Migrations.

IT has been shown in Chapter III that from the point of view of kinship organisations Australia falls into three main areas—occupied by the classless two-phratry, the four-class and the eight-class organisations. The total number of phratry names, thirty-three pairs in all, does not of course fall solely to the count of the two-phratry tribes, but is divided between the three kinds of organisation, the two-phratry having twelve pairs with one anomalous area, the four-class sixteen, and the eight-class five such sets. As regards the relative size of the areas thus organised, the largest seems to be that occupied by the Matteri-Kiraru system, though the Muquara-Kilpara (5) probably runs it close, especially if we take into account the names of like meaning (1–4) in the East Victorian area. The remainder of the two-phratry systems do not range over a wide extent of country, so far as is known; but 10, 11, and 33 are of unknown extent.

In the four-class area are two extensive systems, ranking next after those of South Australia and N.S. Wales; these are Mallera-Wuthera (27) and Pakoota-Wootaro (29); they have a single phratry name in common, which is also found in two other systems; if we add these together, as we may perhaps do on this evidence of a common basis, we have by far the largest phratric system in Australia as the result. Almost equal in extent to either of the two areas occupied by 27 and 29 is that claimed by the better known Kamilaroi system—Dilbi-Kupathin, which spreads over a long, comparatively narrow region, but had possibly at one time a wider field from which at the present time only the corresponding class names can be recovered. Of the remaining thirteen in the two-class region, only 28, one of the Wuthera systems already mentioned, has more than a restricted field of influence. Of moderate size are the four areas in the eight-class system proper, that of the Mara being small in comparison.

Taking now the native names, we find that, in addition to the Wuthera (Ootaroo) sets already mentioned, the Dieri and Kurnandaburi have Matteri (Mattera) in common, while the latter have in the Baddieri tribe a neighbour which shares the Yungo phratry name with them. The fact, if correct, that with the Badieri Yungo is associated with Wutheru, and takes the place of the more usual Yungaru, suggests that we may equate the latter with Yungo. In the eight-class area Uluuru is common to two systems, while a third has Wiliuku, and the fourth Illitchi, all of which seem to be allied, if we may take it that uru, uku, and tchi are suffixes; that they are is borne out by the corresponding names Liaritchi and Liaraku. Other possible equations are Mukula—Mukumurra, and Cheepa—Koocheebinga, but in the latter case, even if koo is a prefix, the distance of the two systems makes any such correspondence improbable. In Victoria the Malian-Multa equation is indisputable; it is interesting to note that the former is found in N.S. Wales as the name of the bird, while Multa belongs to Yorke Peninsula.

As regards the meaning of these names. we find that of the fifty-eight names which remain after deducting those which occur in more than one system, nineteen can be translated with certainty, and we can guess at the meaning of some half dozen more. Of translateable names the most widely spread are various titles of Eaglehawk and Crow, which appear in five different systems in Victoria and New South Wales[1]. Crow reappears in West Australia under the name of Wartung, with white cockatoo, also a Victorian phratry name, as its fellow. In North Queensland, as a parallel to the black and white cockatoo of the south,

[1] For references, meanings, etc. see chap. IV.

we find on the Annan River two species of bee giving their names to phratries; and the Black Duck phratry of the Waradjeri suggests that here too might be found another contrasting pair, if we could translate the other name. For the Euahlayi phratry names, on which more will be said in discussing the "blood" organisations, Mrs Parker gives the translation "Light-blooded" and "Dark-blooded," which comes near that suggested by Mr Mathews—slow and quick blooded. In the Ulu, Illi, and Wili of Northern Territory we seem to recognise Welu (curlew). Koolpuru (emu), Yungaru and Yungo (kangaroo), and Wutheroo (emu) are also possible meanings.

The problems raised by the phratriac nomenclature are complex and probably insoluble. They are in part bound up with the problem of the origin of the organisation itself; of this nature, for example, is the question whether the names correspond to anything existing in the pre-phratriac stage, or whether the organisation was borrowed and the names taken over translated or untranslated into the idiom of the borrowers. If the latter be the solution, we have a simple explanation of the wide-spread Eaglehawk-Crow system as well as of other facts, to which reference is made below.

If on the other hand the names have not been much spread by borrowing,—and the increasing number of small phratry areas known to us tells in favour of this, though it also suggests that the widely-found systems have gained ground at the expense of their neighbours,—then we obviously need some theory as to the origin of the organisation, before we can frame any hypothesis as to the origin of the names.

The prominent part, however, played by the Eaglehawk among phratry names raises some questions which can be discussed on their merits. One of these is the age of phratry names. Some of the earliest records of initiation ceremonies in New South Wales mention that the eaglehawk figured in them[1]. In West Australia this bird is the demiurge, and the progenitors of the phratries, of which crow is one, are his nephews. This is not the only case in which these birds figure in mythology.

[1] See *Man* 1905, no. 28.

As the Rev. John Mathew has pointed out in his work, *Eaglehawk and Crow*, there are found in Australia, especially in the south-eastern portion, a number of myths relating to the conflicts of these birds. These myths he interprets as echoes of a long-past conflict between the aboriginal Negrito race and the invading Papuans, and traces the origin of the phratries to the same racial strife. As an explanation of exogamy the hypothesis is clearly insufficient, but it is evident that no theory of the origin of the phratries can leave exogamy out of the question. The point, however, with which we are immediately concerned is the myth on which in the main Mr Mathew based his theory. Unfortunately, he did not think it necessary to attempt to define either the area covered by the different phratry names—an omission which is remedied by the present work—nor yet the limits within which the myth in question or its analogues are part of the native mythology. These analogues to the story of the battle of Eaglehawk and Crow, ended in the Darling area according to tradition by a treaty between the contending birds, are myths in which birds are said to have destroyed the human race, or a large portion of it, to have contended with Baiame, or one of the other gods, or to have figured in some other conflict[1]. The bird of this myth—the bird conflict myth, as it may be termed—is the Eaglehawk. Possibly, as I have pointed out in the note in *Man*, both bird conflict myths and Eaglehawk-Crow myths—they may be termed collectively bird myths—may go back to a common origin. So far as Mr Mathew's evidence goes, bird myths do not seem to be told outside the colony of Victoria and the Darling area of New South Wales.

A little research, however, shows that this idea is altogether erroneous. There are unfortunately large areas in Australia, as to the mythology of which we know absolutely nothing. Therefore it must not be supposed that the bird conflict myth is confined to the districts in which we have evidence of its existence. We may rather infer that a myth so widely distributed—it ranges from the head of the Bight, 129° E., to the coast north of Sydney, and probably as far as Moreton Bay;

[1] Cf. *Man*, 1905, no. 28.

to the north it is found among the Urabunna, and probably elsewhere—is common property of the Australian Tribes.

A glance at the map will show that the eaglehawk and crow myth covers but a small portion of the area in which the bird conflict myth is found. On the other hand we find within the eaglehawk-crow myth district the phratry names Cockatoo, three names of unknown meaning, and the doubtful Kiraru—Kirarawa. Now if a racial conflict is indicated by the names eaglehawk and crow, this must be either because the contending races were already known by these names, or because the two birds in question are proverbially hostile to each other. In either case we are left without any explanation of the two cockatoo phratries. It may indeed be argued that the locality in which the eaglehawk-crow phratry names are found tells strongly in favour of the racial conflict hypothesis; for it is precisely in this area that the last stand of the aborigines against the invaders may, on the theory put forward by Mr Mathew and accepted by some anthropologists[1], be supposed to have taken place. But against this must be set the fact that in this area also we find two cockatoos, and on the Annan River two bees, arrayed against one another; unless it can be shown that these two birds are also proverbial foes, or that the Australian native had reached a point in his biological investigations at which he recognised that the presence of two closely allied species in a district involves a particularly keen struggle for existence (which they would, however, regard in such an advanced stage of knowledge as appropriate to the designation of intra-racial rather than inter-racial feuds), the two sets of facts balance one another, and leave us still engaged in a vain quest for a conclusion.

Putting theories as to racial conflicts aside, and dealing with the facts as we find them, we seem to have a choice of two hypotheses. Either the eaglehawk-crow myths were told before the phratry names came into existence, or they were invented to explain the existence of the phratry names. Let us assume that none of the unknown names mean eaglehawk or crow, and that the eaglehawk-crow area has remained approximately the

[1] But see *J. R. S. Vict.* XVII, 120.

same size, or has, at any rate, not diminished (excluding, of course, those cases where it seems to have lost ground owing to the disappearance of phratry names altogether, as among the Kurnai); we must then, on the second theory, assume that the story of the combat spread to tribes with completely different phratry names like the Urabunna, and got mixed up with their ceremonies of initiation (the most sacred part of the mythology of the Australian natives, and one not likely to be much influenced by chance intruders); and that it came even in some cases to be told of Baiame, the creator and institutor of the rites of initiation, who is represented as himself taking part in the conflict and gaining a victory over the foes of mankind[1]. On the whole, therefore, this view of the case appears improbable.

To the theory that the Eaglehawk-Crow story was originally independent of the phratry names no such objections apply. We are indefinitely remote from the period at which the anthropologist will be able to do for Australia what Franz Boas has done for the North-West of America—draw up a table showing the resemblances and differences between the stock of folktales of the different tribes, or, which is more important for our present purpose, of the main divisions, eastern, central, and western, which the analysis of initiation ceremonies gives us—a tripartite division which Curr also makes on the linguistic side, though Mathew's map shows considerable intermixture in this respect. Until we know to what extent the Urabunna or the Ikula have folktales in common with the Victorian area, or,—which is perhaps more important, though we do not seem to hear of any communication on this line,—how far there is a stock of folktales common to the Darling district and the central area, it is obviously idle to speculate as to how it comes that an Eaglehawk myth is told in both areas. The physical anthropology of the Australian natives is at present a little-worked field, in which, singularly enough, the French have done more than the English, to our shame be it said. Possibly a somatological survey might disclose to what extent the central tribes are distinct from the eastern group, and how far we may assume movements of

[1] See *Man*, 1905, no. 28, where I show that in the Wellington Valley was current a myth of the conflict between Baiame and Mudgegong (=Eaglehawk).

population, subsequent to the original peopling of the country by the stocks in question, in either or both directions. In the absence of such data, and until an Australian Grimm has arisen to bring order into the present linguistic chaos, the evidence from folktales seems to promise most light on the question of migrations.

We are, of course, confronted by the difficulty that this evidence may simply disclose the lines along which tribal intercommunication has been most easy, whether in the way of simple interchange of commodities, evidence of which we have over considerable areas in Australia, or in the way of intermarriage, which, as we see by the example of the Urabunna and the Arunta, is found in spite of fundamental differences of tribal organisation. A common stock of folktales due to this cause would leave unexplained the prominence of the bird myth in the sacred rites, and leave the present hypothesis, in this regard, on a par with that of post-phratriac dissemination, in respect of probability. On the other hand we have the Scylla of tribal property in land, an idea so firmly rooted in our own day in the minds of the Australians as to make wars of conquest unthinkable to them, and to transform the practical part of their intertribal feuds into mere raids. If, therefore, investigation showed that the central and eastern tribes are in possession of a stock of folktales with many items in common, we should always have to take into consideration the possibility that these tales antedate the complete occupation of Australia, and go back to a period when the eastern and central divisions were in close relation. The probability of this view would, of course, depend on the extent of the resemblance between the two stocks of tales, or, perhaps, rather on the extent of the resemblance between those tales which they have in common; for it is clear that a close resemblance between comparatively few items would be more effective proof of intercommunication than a less marked general resemblance between the tale-stocks as a whole.

In spite of the deficiencies of our evidence we may perhaps incline to the view that the bird myth dates back to a very early period. Until it has been shown that intrusive elements are not only taken up into the tribal stock of tales, but also incorporated in the more sacred portion of those tales, which are told at the tribal mysteries, it will always remain more probable that the myth belongs to the two divisions as a result of lineal and not lateral transmission. If this is so the differences between the initiation ceremonies, no less than the anthropomorphic form of the myth in the eastern division, as compared with the purely theriomorphic story of the central division and the mixed form of the Ikula, will enable us to say that the period when the separation of the divisions took place must be very remote.

There is, therefore, no inherent improbability in supposing that the bird myth was told before the phratry names were invented or adopted, and that the latter were in some cases taken from the principal characters in the myth. This conclusion is supported by the fact that the phratry names seem to be subsequent to the present grouping, if we may take as our guide the fact that the frontiers of the phratry names correspond with the boundaries between the central and eastern divisions. The fact that there is a cross division, if we base our reasoning on the class organisation, need not of course be taken into account, for we have every reason to believe that the classes are subsequent to the phratries.

In favour of the derivation of the phratry names from the myth tells also the five-fold division of the eaglehawk-crow groups into Muquara and Kilpara, Bunjil and Waa, Merung and Yuckembruk, Multa or Malian and Umbe. For it is clearly more probable that the names should have been taken from a common object than that they should have been in their origin identical in form and subsequently differentiated, as the languages changed; we have in fact direct evidence of a tendency to preserve the old names, which we may perhaps regard as the sacred names, after the bird has been rebaptised in the terminology of daily life. Over and above this we have of course the fact that the sacred language has, generally speaking, both in Australia and elsewhere, this unchanging character. But this simple name-borrowing theory, it is clear, is equally valid as an explanation of the facts.

Although we cannot determine the meaning of the names

the quadripartite division of the Mallera-Wuthera[1] and allied phratries in the north is evidence of a similar tendency. It is by no means impossible that Mallera, Yungaroo, and Pakoota all mean the same thing. (This ignorance of the meaning of the phratry and class names is *primâ facie* evidence of their high antiquity.) In the newly-discovered phratry names of the eight-class tribes we have yet another instance of tripartite division. If we may assume that Illitchi, Uluuru, and Wiliuku are from the same root (which, as we have seen, is probably *welu*, the terminations *-uku*, *-itchi*, and *-uru* (= *-aree*) being formative suffixes), we have here too a single phratry name on the one side and three sister names on the other. While it is clear that the names cannot be in any sense of the term recent, from the fact that linguistic differentiation had already gone some distance in what we may call, for want of a better term, groups speaking a stock language (in proof of which we have only to look at the formative suffixes), it seems equally clear that the present phratry names must be considerably later than the final settlement of the country. At the same time it must not be forgotten that the existence of numerous small phratries, the number of which may yet be largely increased by more exact research, is *primâ facie* a proof that the groups which adopted them had not reached the stage at which anything like that tribal (still less national) organisation was known, which is at the present day characteristic of the Arunta, and, perhaps, we may say, of all groups organised on a class system with class names known and used over an area far beyond that over which the (in a restricted sense) tribal language extends.

The recurrence of crow in the phratry name of the far west lends further support to the view that the phratry names were selected in some way, and were not due to some accident of savage wit. The view has been taken that the phratry animals were originally totems, or animals that became totems at a later stage. In view of the large number of totems found in many tribes, or even restricting their number to six or eight in each phratry, it is not difficult to estimate the probability that cockatoo and crow would recur in different areas, and that

[1] Chap. IV, phratries, nos. 27—29.

an opposition of characters should be found in other cases. The hypothesis needs at any rate to be combined with a theory, firstly, of borrowing of phratry names, a process which must indeed have played a large part in the development of the present system, but which does not necessarily involve the supposition that the borrowed names replaced previously existing home-made names; and, secondly, of selection of such names as were not borrowed.

It has been mentioned that the principle of tribal property in land or, to be strictly accurate, in hunting grounds, is, at the present day, a fundamental one in native Australian jurisprudence. But, as is shown by the map, in some cases the phratries are split into two or more segments[1], more or less remote from one another, geographically speaking. Now this apparent segmentation must be due to migration; it can hardly arise from the chance adoption of identical names; for the groups in which the names occur are, though separated by a considerable distance, not so remote as, on the theory of chance selection, we should expect them to be, in other words the probability is in favour of the segmentation of an original group or its cleavage by an intrusive element. Of the causes of this drift of population, which on a large scale, and under pressure of any kind, might well overrule even the rights of property, we have naturally no idea. In a homogeneous mass like the population of Australia, and especially in a mass whose level of culture is so low as to leave no remains behind which we could use for the purposes of chronology, it is hopeless to expect any solution of any of the problems connected with drift of population. One thing only seems clear, and on this point we may hope for some light from the data of philology, namely that the migration was long subsequent to the original *Völkerwanderung*; for this must have preceded the rise of phratry names, which again must have preceded the migration of which the segmentation of groups, evidenced by the names themselves, is at present, and in default of the aid of philology, our only proof.

The migrations of which we are speaking must, if the possession of one phratry name in common be worth anything

[1] See Map III, phratry no. 28.

as evidence of a closer connection between the groups, have been internal to a group or, if the term be preferred, to a nation occupying the south of Queensland. For in the absence of evidence that phratry names are to be found outside their own linguistic groups, we cannot but infer from the quadripartite division of the Wuthera phratries both the linguistic unity (and language must be in Australia the ultimate test of racial relationship on a large scale) and the internal movements of the group in which they occur.

In favour of the primitive unity of the Wuthera groups, is the fact that with small exceptions, and those on the outskirts of the district, the area occupied by the assumed homogeneous pre-phratry group has the same class names throughout—which is at the same time a proof that the class names are posterior to the phratry names ; for the later the date, the more extensive the group, may be taken to be the rule in savage communities ; if the phratry names came later than the class names we should expect them to be identical, and the class names different instead of the reverse. But to the relative age of classes and phratries we return at another point of our argument.

The available data being few, it could hardly be expected that a discussion of them would be very fruitful. In the present chapter we have, however, shown that the phratry names and organisation are probably of very early date, that considerable movements of population took place within the linguistic groups subsequent to the adoption of the phratry names, and that these names have been selected for some explicit reason and not adopted at haphazard.

# CHAPTER VI.

## ORIGIN OF PHRATRIES.

Mr Lang's theory and its basis. Borrowing of phratry names. Split groups. The Victorian area. Totems and phratry names. Reformation theory of phratriac origin.

IF a pre-phratry organisation developed into the system as we find it, it is a little difficult to see how selection can have operated, unless, indeed, as Mr Lang suggests, the phratries are *transformed* connubial groups, in which case they may have received new names. It is perhaps simpler to suppose that the cases of selection of phratry names cited above are those in which the organisation has been borrowed with full knowledge of its meaning. If this view is correct, no criticism of theories of the origin of phratries is possible from the point of view of the names actually existing, for we cannot say which, if any, are those which were evolved in the organisation which served as a model to the remainder.

Broadly speaking the theories of origin at present in the field may be reduced to two: in the first place, the conscious reformation theory, which supposes that man discovered the evils of in-and-in breeding, a point on which some discussion will be found in a later portion of this work. In the second place, there is the unconscious evolution theory put forward by Mr Lang, whose criticism of the opposing view makes it unnecessary to deal with the objections here[1].

Mr Lang's original theory took for its basis the hypothesis, put forward by the late Mr J. J. Atkinson, in *Primal Law*, of

[1] *Secret of the Totem*, pp. 31, 91 sq.

the origin of exogamy. His starting-point was mankind in the brute stage. At the point in the evolution of the human race at which Mr Atkinson takes up his tale, man, or rather Eoanthropos, was, according to his conjecture, organised, if that term can be applied to the grouping of the lower animals, in bodies consisting of one adult male, an attendant horde of adult females, including, probably, at any rate after a certain lapse of time, his own progeny, together with the immature offspring of both sexes. As the young males came to maturity, they would be expelled from the herd, as is actually the case with cattle and other mammals, by their sire, now become their foe. They probably wandered about, as do the young males of some existing species, in droves of a dozen or more, and at certain seasons of the year, one or more of them would, as they felt their powers mature, engage the lord of their own or of another herd in single combat, until with the lapse of time the latter either succumbed or was driven from the herd to end his days in solitary ferocity, his hand against everyone, just as we see the rogue elephant wage war indiscriminately on all who approach him.

In process of time, so Mr Atkinson suggests, with the lengthening childhood conditioned by the progress of the race, maternal love of a more enduring kind developed, than is found among the non-human species of the present day. This led eventually to the presence of a young male, perhaps the youngest born of a given mother, being permitted to remain, on conditions, in the herd after he had attained maturity. The original lord and master of the herd retained, Mr Atkinson supposes, his full sovereignty over the females born in the herd as well as over those whom his prowess had perhaps added to it from time to time. The young male on the other hand was not condemned to a life of celibacy as a condition of his non-enforcement of the traditional decree of banishment. He was permitted to find a mate, but she must be a mate not born in the herd, nor one of the harem of his sire; he had, if he wished to wed, to capture a spouse for himself from another herd. For the detailed working out of this ingenious theory we must refer our readers to Mr Atkinson's work, *Primal Law*. Here it suffices to state the primal law which resulted from the process sketched above. This primal law was "thou shalt not marry within the group." This law, at first enforced by the superior strength of the sire, came in the process of time to be a traditional rule of conduct, almost an instinct. And with this we reach the theory put forward in *Social Origins* by Mr Andrew Lang, according to which local groups received animal names, perhaps from their neighbours. These local groups being exogamous for the reason just given, and the group name being eventually[1] given, not only to the actual members of the group, but also to the women, captured or otherwise, who became the mates of the men of the adjoining groups, it necessarily resulted that the men of a group, so long as the mother's group name did not descend to her children, were of one name, while their wives were of another, or more probably of many other names. The group became definitely heterogeneous when the maternal group name descended to the children born in the alien group, and in process of time these maternal group names became totem names.

Meanwhile the original group names had been retained and applied, along with the totem or quasi-totem names, to the members of the group; the name being probably, in the first place, that of the group in which they were born, but, with the rise of the matrilineal descent, which has been discussed above, eventually taken from the group to which the mother belonged.

During these processes the custom had sprung up to select a wife, not at random from any of the probably more or less hostile surrounding groups, but from one particular group with which the group of the candidate for matrimony had in the course of time come to be on friendly terms.

The names of these two groups, which drew in other smaller groups, became the phratry names of the newly-formed aggregate, the largest unit known to primitive society at that stage of its evolution, and corresponding roughly to what we have defined as a tribe; for it was united by bonds of friendship, and in the course of time the language, originally very different no doubt, how different we can, indeed, hardly say,

[1] Mr Lang's view is that the women from the first retained their original group names wherever they went. *Letter of July 27th*, 1906.

must have so far coalesced, owing to the interchange of wives (in so far as a distinct woman's language, traces of which are found among some savage tribes, was not developed), as to produce a single tongue.

This theory Mr Lang has now fortified and elaborated in *The Secret of the Totem*, the most important new point being the demonstration of the fact that totem kins which bear names of the same significance as the phratry names are almost invariably in the eponymous phratries—a clear proof that law and not chance has determined their position.

As an explanation of the distribution of phratry names Mr Lang adopts a theory which combines the hypotheses of evolution and borrowing, and thus explains both the wide area covered by some systems, and the increasing multitude of organisations confined to small districts, which more minute research reveals. This does not, it is true, explain the geographical remoteness of different parts of the same system or of allied systems, shown to be so by the identity of phratry animal or name. Not only is Wuthera-Mallera split into two sections; but a portion of Wuthera-Yungaru seems to be in the same position; if we may take the Badieri Yungo as equivalent to Yungaru, dispersion alone suffices to explain the case; but if Yungo is derived from the Kurnandaburi, who have Mattera as the sister phratry, then we have the Badieri phratry names borrowed each from a different tribe, at any rate in appearance.

In reality this state of things affords the strongest possible support to Mr Lang's hypothesis, if only we can suppose that the formation of tribes is subsequent to the elaboration of the phratriac system. For it might well happen that an original Yungo local group divided, from economic causes, but that each half retained its original name. Under these circumstances the two portions formed connubial alliances with other groups; and in the tribes as we see the names of these split groups are found as phratry names, combined in each case with a different sister phratry name. We find for example Wuthera-Yungo, Yungo-Mattera, Matteri-Kiraru in the central area. The same theory will explain the appearance of Wuthera beside three other sister names, though here we must call in the borrowing and migration theories as well, to explain the wide area over which the names are found. We have seen that in the northern tribes one of the phratry names appears to be in each case from the same root; if this is so, we can apply to them too the split-group hypothesis.

The case of Eaglehawk-Crow is less simple. Separated from the Darling area by a considerable space lie four systems of the same name in the east of Victoria. Here it is hardly possible to assume that the latter systems have migrated; on the other hand the area covered by the Darling group suggests that it is unlikely to have been forced from its original home by pressure from outside. Perhaps it is simplest to suppose that the Wiradjeri have gradually forced their way in, wedge fashion, between the different sections, and either swallowed up the intervening members or driven them before them; this would account for the existence of the anomalous groups to the southwest.

In this area, too, we seem to have a case of the split group; but the identity of meaning of the other phratry names (Malian and Multa both mean Eaglehawk) makes it clear that it is simply a case of translation—a possibility which must be kept in mind in the other cases also. It is a common phenomenon for two tribes to have the name of one animal in common, while for that of another entirely different words are in use. The four Victorian groups appear to have borrowed the phratry names, but the centre from which they took them must remain uncertain.

It may be noted in passing that the view of Prof. Gregory, who holds that the occupation of Victoria by the blacks dates back no more than 300 years, is hardly borne out by the distribution of the phratriac systems. It is clearly improbable that they were developed *in situ*, for this would make the organisation of very much more recent date than we have any warrant for supposing. On the other hand it is improbable that four tribes, all with the same phratriac names, should have taken their course in the same direction, and settled in proximity to one another, at any rate, unless the natural features of the country made this course the only possible one.

To return to Mr Lang's theory, it obviously suggests, if it does not demand, that such phratries as are spread over wide areas should in the main follow the lines of linguistic or cultural areas. Our knowledge of these is hardly sufficient to enable us to say at present how far the presumption of coincidence is fulfilled; but it is certain that in more than one large area the facts are as Mr Lang's theory requires them to be.

On the other hand in New South Wales we find an area in which we fail to discern the lines on which the phratriac systems are distributed. Here, however, we are at a disadvantage in consequence of the uncertainty introduced by the unsettled question of "blood" organisations[1]. Further research may show that the supposed phratriac areas, which are apparently only portions of the Wiradjeri territory, are in reality to be assigned to the "blood" organisations, which we may probably assign to a later date than the phratries and classes.

Perhaps Mr Lang's theory hardly accounts for the fact that eaglehawk and crow figure not only as phratry names but also in the myths and rites. It is not apparent why eaglehawk and crow groups should take the lead and give their names to the phratries unless it was as contrasted colours; on the other hand, if they were selected as the names from among a number of others this difficulty vanishes, but then we do not see why these names are not more widely found, unless indeed the untranslated names mean eaglehawk and crow; but possibly all express a contrast of some sort.

On the whole, however, it may be said that Mr Lang's theory holds the field. Not only is it internally consistent, which cannot be affirmed of the reformation theory, but it colligates the facts far better. This may be illustrated by a single point.

On the reformation theory, unaccompanied, as it is, by any hypothesis of borrowing of phratry names, we should *primâ facie* find the latter, where they are translateable, to be those of the animals which are most frequently found as totems. Now in the area covered by Dr Howitt's recent work, omitting those tribes for which our lists of totems are admittedly not complete,

[1] See pp. 31, 50.

we find that emu, kangaroo, snake, eaglehawk, and iguana are found as totems in about two-thirds of the cases; then, after a long interval, come wallaby and crow, less than half as often, with opossum rather more frequently, in half the total number. But it is clearly outside the bounds of probability that four of the commonest totems should not give their names, so far as is known, to phratries, while eaglehawk recurs five, crow six, and cockatoo three times, the two latter in one case in a remote area. Not only so, but the opposition between the phratry names—black and white or the like—is unintelligible, if, as on Dr Durkheim's theory, the phratries are simply the elementary totem groups which intermarried and threw off secondary totem kins. But criticism of other theories opens a wide field, into which it is best not to diverge.

On the development theory the phratries came into existence perhaps as the result of the persistence of an old custom of exogamy, non-moral in its inception, or, it may be, as a result of the rise of totemic tabus. The reformation theory, on the other hand, makes the conscious attainment of a better state of society the object of the institution of a dichotomous organisation. It will therefore be well to see what results in practice from the phratriac organisation.

In the two-phratry area (other rules, which usually exist, apart) it is impossible for children of the same mother or father, or of sisters or of brothers, to marry, nor can one of the parents, either mother or father, according to the rule of descent, take her or his own child in marriage. Now if the object of the reformation was to prevent parents from marrying children, it was clearly not attained. If, on the other hand, it was intended to prevent children of the same mother or father from intermarrying, the result could have been attained far more simply, either by direct prohibition, such as is found in other cases, or by the institution of totemic exogamy, which, in the view of some authorities, already existed, and consequently made the phratry superfluous.

According to Dr Frazer's 1905 theory, phratries were introduced to prevent brother and sister marriage and exogamous bars began in the female line[1]. Against this hypothesis may be

[1] *Fortn. Rev.* LXXVIII, 459.

urged not only the objections first stated but also the fact that for Dr Frazer the Arunta are primitive and yet reckon descent (of the class) in the *male* line. If, as he conceives, conceptional totemism was transformed in the central tribes into patrilineal totemism, I fail to see why the phratries or classes should descend in the female line.

If in the third place, it was proposed to prevent children of sisters or of brothers from intermarrying, it is completely mysterious why children of brothers and sisters should not only not have been prevented in the same way, but absolutely be regarded as the proper mates for each other. Even if a single community reformed itself on these lines, it is hardly conceivable that many should have done so, even if we suppose that the advantages of prohibition were preached from tribe to tribe by missionaries of the new order of things. *Ex hypothesi*, cousin marriage was not regarded as harmful; and it is highly improbable that any people in the lower stages of culture should have discovered that in-and-in breeding is harmful, for the results, especially in a people which contained no degenerates, would not appear at once, even if they appeared at all.

On this point therefore the probabilities are wholly on the side of development as against reformation.

An additional reason against the reformation theory is found in the fact that phratries, on this theory, would never exceed two in number, but in practice there are, as shown in Chapter II, wide variations.

# CHAPTER VII.

## CLASS NAMES.

Classes later than Phratries. Anomalous Phratry Areas. Four-class Systems. Borrowing of Names. Eight-class System. Resemblances and Differences of Names. Place of Origin. Formative Elements of the Names: Suffixes, Prefixes. Meanings of the Class Names.

THE priority of phratries over classes is commonly admitted and it is unnecessary to argue the question at length. The main grounds for the assumption are: (1) that it is *a priori* probable that the fourfold division succeeded the twofold division, exactly as the eightfold division has succeeded, and apparently is still gaining ground, at the expense of the four-class system. (2) Over a considerable and compact area phratries alone are found without a trace of named classes, if we except the anomalous organisation recorded by Dawson in S. W. Victoria. On the other hand, while we find certain tribes among whom no phratry names have yet been discovered, it is inherently probable that this is due to their having been forgotten and not to their never having existed. It is possible that the encroachments of an alien class system have in some cases helped on the extinction of the phratry names. (3) We find classes without phratry names, not in a compact group, but scattered up and down more or less at random, suggesting that chance and not law has been at work to produce this result. (4) Where class names are found without corresponding phratry names, they are invariably arranged in what may be termed anonymous phratries; that is to say, in pairs or fours, so that the member of one class is under normal circumstances not at liberty to select a wife at will from the other three, but is usually limited to one of the other classes. This state of things clearly points to a time when the phratries were recognised by the tribes in question.

(5) While the classes are arranged in pairs or fours, according to whether the system is four- or eight-class, the totems, on the other hand, are distributed phratry fashion; in other words, one group of totems belongs to each pair or quadruplet of classes. This divergent organisation of the classes (four or eight for the whole tribe) and totems (two groups for the whole tribe) can only be explained on the supposition that the phratry everywhere preceded the class organisation.

The spatial relations of the phratries and classes are sufficiently clear from the map; and a table shows how far cross divisions are found.

The main area of disturbance of the normal relations is, as shown in Table IV (p. 51), the district occupied by the Koorgilla class-system and its immediate neighbourhood. The Yungaroo-Witteru group has three representatives in the Koorgilla class and one in the Kurpal class. The Pakoota-Wootaroo phratry has likewise three in the Koorgilla class, a fourth being in the Yowingo organisation. A large area is occupied by the Mallera-Witteru phratry in the Koorgilla class, and one tribe is again found in the Yowingo group. No class names are recorded for the Undekerebina in the Pakoota group, and no phratry names for the Mycoolon and Workobongo in the Yowingo group, nor for the Yerunthully in the Koorgilla group, which in addition to tribes belonging to the three Wuthera phratries also embraces within its limits the small Purgoma and Jouon tribes.

The only other anomaly recorded in addition to those mentioned is among the tribes on the south and south-east of the area just dealt with, which have the Barang class names with the Kamilaroi phratry names, or the Kamilaroi class names with tribal phratry names. In four cases therefore the phratry is found outside the limits of the class usually associated with it, or, in other words, it is associated with a strange class system. In one case, that of the Kalkadoon, this is sufficiently explained by the fact that the tribe is itself now remote geographically speaking from its fellows, owing to the interposition of Pitta-Pitta and allied tribes. In the other three cases the facts seem to point to a change in the intertribal relationships in the period intervening between the adoption of phratry names and the introduction of the class system. If the lines of intercourse and intermarriage had suffered a revolution in the interval, the names, the origin of which we have yet to consider, would naturally show a different grouping of the tribes; for it is on the grouping of the tribes that the spread of the names, whether of phratries or classes, must have depended.

The main mass of the tribes organised on the four-class system lies in Queensland and New South Wales, and whereas only two sets of names are found in the latter colony, no less than fifteen (some of which are, however, of more than doubtful authenticity) are reported from various parts of Queensland. From Northern Territory two (Anula and Mara) of small extent are reported[1]; a considerable area of this colony, as well as of South and West Australia, is occupied by the Arunta system, and the closely allied classes to the north-west of them. The only other four-class system in West Australia of which we have definite information is that west and north of King George's Sound and eastwards for an unknown distance.

Covering nearly the whole of New South Wales outside the area occupied by the two-phratry tribes of the Darling country, and extending far up into Queensland, we find the well-known Muri-Kubbi, Ippai-Kumbo classes (1) of the Kamilaroi nation[2]. The Kamilaroi system appears to have touched the sea in the neighbourhood of Sydney. According to Mr Mathews, the Darkinung, who inhabited this part of New South Wales, substituted Bya for Muri. (1*a*) In like manner the Wiradjeri are stated by Gribble to have replaced Kumbo by Wombee; this may however be no more than a dialectical variant.

Lying along the sea coast north-east of the Darkinung and east of the main mass of Kamilaroi tribe were the Kombinegherry and other tribes, whom Mr Mathews denominates the Anaywan. Their classes are given by him as Irrpoong, Marroong, Imboong, and Irrong; but an earlier authority

[1] In practice they are eight-class. [2] The numbers refer to those used in chapter IV.

gives the forms Kurbo, Marro, Wombo, and Wirro (2); at Wide Bay we find Baran, Balkun, Derwen, and Bundar (3) with an alternative form Banjoor.

North of them, still on the coast, we find the Kuinmurbura with Kurpal, Kuialla, Karilbura, and Munal (4); for the Taroombul, which I am unable to locate, Mr Mathews gives Koodala in place of Kuialla and Karalbara for Karilbura. For the Kangoollo, lying inland from this group, Mr Mathews gives Kearra, Banjoor, Banniar, and Koorpal. This suggests that there is some confusion, for the names include two from 4, and one or two from 3.

A very large area is occupied by tribes with the classes (5) Koorgila, Bunburi, Wunggo, and Obur (and variants). They include the Yuipera and allied tribes, the Kogai, the Wakelbura and allied tribes, the Yambeena, the Yerunthully, the Woonamurra, the Mittakoodi, the Pitta-Pitta, etc., together with the Purgoma of the Palm Islands and the neighbouring Jouon, whose headquarters are at Cooktown. In the southern portion of this group a correspondent of Curr's has reported the classes Nullum, Yoolgo, Bungumbura, and Teilling. We have class names analogous in form to the third of these names, it is true, but it resembles tribal names so closely as to suggest that the observer in question was really referring to a tribe and not to a class. If this is so we may perhaps identify Teilling with the Toolginbura. There seems to be no reason for admitting these four names to a place among the other groups of class names. In like manner we may dismiss the class names assigned to the Yukkaburra by an inaccurate correspondent of Curr's, who gives Utheroo, Multheroo, Yungaroo, and Goorgilla. It seems clear that the first and third of these are really phratry names; possibly the second is a dialectical form for Utheroo.

From Halifax Bay and Hinchinbrook Island are reported the names Korkoro, Korkeen, Wongo, and Wotero (with variants). Among the Joongoongie of North Queensland we find Langenam, Namegoor, Packewicky, and Pamarung (15); and among the Karandee Curr gives an anomalous and probably defective set, Moorob, Heyanbo, Lenai, Roanga, and Yelet.

The Goothanto and Wollungurma have Ranya, Rara, Loora, and Awunga (8); allied to these perhaps are the Jury, Ararey, Barry, and Mungilly of the Koogobathy; the Ahjeerena, Arrenynung, Perrynung, and Mahngal of the Koonjan are clearly variants of the latter set. East of the Koogobathy lie the Warkeman with Koopungie, Kellungie, Chukungie, and Karpungie (6), with an allied tribe on the Tully River with classes, Kurongon, Kurkulla, Chikun, Karavangie, the two latter obviously corresponding to Warkeman classes, the second to Koorgilla.

The Miappe, Mycoolon, Kalkadoon, and Workoboongo have Youingo, Maringo, Badingo, and Jimmilingo (9), with alternatives Kapoodingo, Kungilingo, and Toonbeungo.

The Yoolanlanya and others have Deringara, Gubilla, Koomara, and Belthara, possibly a defective list, for Mr Mathews adds to these for the Ullayilinya Lookwara and Ungella (probably a defective set) in another communication. Two of these are obviously identical with the Arunta Koomara and Bulthara, with which are associated Purula and Panungka (13), while Ungilla and Gubilla are taken from the eight-class system to which we may probably assign the tribe. North-west of the Arunta, outside the eight-class area, the class names are almost identical with, though they differ widely in form from the Arunta names. They are Burong, Ballieri, Baniker, and Caiemurra (13). The form Boorgarloo is given as a variant. Mrs Bates has found a system (14) in S.W. Australia.

On the western shores of the Gulf of Carpentaria we find the Mara with Purdal, Murungun, Mumbali, and Kuial (10); and the Anula with Awukaria, Roumburia, Urtalia, and Wialia (11).

The only two remaining four-class systems of which the names are known are on the Annan River with Wandi, Walar, Jorro, and Kutchal (7)—the Ngarranga of Yorke Peninsula, with Kari, Wani, Wilthi, and Wilthuthu.

Attention has been called in the course of the above exposition to various cases in which the class names found among one group of tribes are in part if not entirely identical with those found among their neighbours. A close examination discloses other possible though hardly probable points of contact besides those already enumerated. The variant form Banjoora in 3 seems to be the same as the Banjoor of the Kangulu, which again has Koorpal in common with 4, and also Kearra, if we may equate the latter with Kuialla. This again is perhaps the Kuial of the Mara tribe (9).

The Marroong of 2 seems to be the Maringo of 9, and we may perhaps also equate the Kurbo of this group with the Kurpal of 4. Irroong resembles the roanga of the Karandee which is probably the Arawongo of the Goothanto.

In 5 Wongo suggests the Youingo of 9; it reappears in the Halifax Bay list, as also does Koorgilla in one of the variants. Again Kubi (1) corresponds to Koobaroo (5), and Kumbo (Wombee) to Bunburi (Unburi), but we can hardly regard them as the same words. Koodalla and Koorpal (4) may be the same as Kellungie and Koopungie (6); the other pair shows no resemblance.

Possibly the Wiradjeri Wombee is the Kombinegherry Wombo; it is at any rate significant that the name is found in the portion of the tribe nearest the Kombinegherry.

We have seen that the Arunta and their north-western neighbours have a four-class system, the component names of which are found with little variation over a range of nearly 25° of longitude. In the forms Kiemarra, Palyeri, Burong, and Baniker, the class names in vogue among the southern Arunta meet us again near the North-West Cape, thus covering a larger area than even the widespread Koorgila-Bunburi class names of Queensland, and forming a striking contrast to the narrow limits of the majority of the four-class system. This peculiarity is reproduced in the compact area of the central eight-class tribes, north and north-east of the Koomara four-class area, though with much greater variations in the names. Bulthara however in the form Palyeri is found in more or less disguised shapes in the whole of the eighteen tribes, whose class names are shown in Table I a; Koomara is found in shapes which are on the whole harder to recognise, and Panunga and Purula in two or three cases, either replaced by another word or so changed as to be unrecognisable. Of the supplementary names belonging to the eight-class Arunta, Uknaria, Ungalla, Appungerta, Umbitchana, Ungalla is found in the whole of the tribes under consideration, and Appungerta undergoes on the whole but little change; Uknaria is practically not found outside the Arunta area, and Umbitchana is in six cases replaced by Yacomary, which seems to be a form of Koomara (to this point we recur later).

Although this suggests that the names were in the first case taken from the Arunta a comparison of them shows that it is not among this tribe that the greatest number of forms common to the whole group and the greatest general resemblance of the names is to be found, as is shown by the comparative tables below. Judged by the standard of resemblance the Oolawunga of the north-west, on the Victoria River, have preserved the names nearest their original forms. Judged by the standard of least deviation from the common stock of names and basing the comparison, not on resemblances but on differences, the Koorangie of the upper waters of the same river take the first place, with the Oolawunga not far behind. In each case the Inchalachee, the most easterly of the group, take the last place, followed in the table of resemblances by the Walpari and the Worgaia; and in the table of differences by the Worgaia and, though at a considerable distance, the Mayoo and the Walpari.

*Figure of Resemblance*[1].

| | |
|---|---|
| Oolawunga | 55 |
| Bingongina | 54 |
| Umbaia | 51 |
| Koorangie | 50 |
| Yookala, Binbinga | 48 |
| Gnanji | 47 |
| Meening | 43 |
| Warramunga, Yungmunni | 41 |
| Arunta, Mayoo | 40 |
| Kaitish, Yungarella, Tjingilli | 39 |
| Worgaia | 37 |
| Walpari | 31 |
| Inchalachee | 28 |

[1] These are merely rough percentages based on arbitrary values for partial resemblances.

*Figure of Difference*[1].

| | |
|---|---|
| Koorangie | 31 |
| Oolawunga | 33 |
| Umbaia | 35 |
| Bingongina | 37 |
| Yungmunni | 42 |
| Gnanji, Tjingilli | 44 |
| Warramunga | 45 |
| Arunta | 46 |
| Binbinga | 49 |
| Yookala | 50 |
| Meening | 52 |
| Kaitish | 54 |
| Yungarella, Walpari | 56 |
| Mayoo | 57 |
| Worgaia | 69 |
| Inchalachee | 84 |

Attention has already been drawn to the resemblance between the Arunta four-class names and the names of the eight-class group. It is clearly of high importance to determine whether the resemblance is on the whole between the names of the western group and the eight-class names, or whether the latter can more readily be derived from those of the Arunta. In the latter case it is obvious that the position of the Oolawunga and Koorangie in the comparative tables is due, not to their having been the tribes from which all the others derived their names, but rather to movements of population subsequent to the adoption of the class names. If on the other hand it appears that the names came in the first instance from the more western portion of the Koomara group, we have some grounds for supposing that the names and the system reached the eight-class area from the west and not from the south.

We have already seen that in the case of Palyeri-Bulthara all the evidence points to the name having come from the west. In the case of Panunga the evidence is weaker, certain of the forms being derivable from either Baniker or Panunga, but with the exception of the Warramunga, and possibly the

[1] This table shows what percentage of names is completely different; partial differences are not allowed for.

Tjingili, there are no tribes of whom we can definitely say that they took the name from the Arunta, whereas there are at least four cases where the resemblance is distinctly with the western class names, and several more in which it can more readily be derived from them. The resemblance between Koomarra and Kiemarra or Kiamba is already considerable, and makes it difficult to estimate the probabilities in most cases; the problem is complicated by the question of prefixes, which will come up for discussion later, and on the whole there appears to be no certain solution of the problem, though the Mayoo seem to have taken over and varied the western form. In the case of Purula-Burong there appear to be indeterminate cases; six seem to tell in favour of a southern origin; three suggest a western origin; and one word Chupil (f. Namilpa) seems to be from a different root.

The problem is further complicated by the anomalous class name Yakomari, to which allusion has already been made. As will be seen later, *cha* or *ja* seem to be prefixes, and if that is so we can hardly avoid the conclusion that Yakomari is Koomara or Kiemara. But in the table it takes the place of Umbitchana, with which it is not even remotely connected philologically; Jamara and its various forms take the place in the table occupied by Koomara among the Arunta when Yakomari holds the eighth place as well as in other cases. If therefore *ku*, *ja*, and *ya* are simply prefixes, as seems to be the case, we have this class name duplicated among five of the tribe—the Umbaia, Yookala, Binbinga, Worgaia, Yangarella, and Inchalachee, of which one comes near the top, and two fairly high in the comparative table. It is however worthy of notice that these six tribes form the eastern group, and are consequently precisely those among which we should, on the hypothesis that the class names originated in the western portion of the area, expect to find the greatest amount of variation and the most numerous anomalies. Dividing the six tribes into two groups, western and eastern, each of three tribes, we find that the cumulative resemblance of the western group to the Arunta is 132, to the Oolawunga 186; the same figures for the eastern group, more remote from the Oolawunga, but practically equidistant with the western group from the Arunta, are 91 and 112. This again seems to lend support to the hypothesis of a western origin. It is perhaps simplest to suppose that the majority of the names came from the west; but that Yakomari, travelling upwards from the south-west, displaced the more usual eighth class name, or perhaps we should say, replaced it, when the eight-class system was adopted, for a name is not likely to have gone out of use when it had once been applied as a designation.

Attention has been called in connection with the phratries to the suffixes such as *um*, *itch*, *aku*[1], etc. Their precise meaning is usually uncertain. An attentive consideration of the class names seems to show that similar suffixes have been used in forming them. If we compare Panunga and Baniker, it seems a fair conclusion that the *ban* or *pan* is compounded with *iker* (*aku*) or *unga*, for among the Yookala, the nearest neighbours of the Bingongina, who have it as a phratriac suffix, the *-agoo* of the class names is unmistakeably independent of the root word, whatever that may be. In addition to *unga* we find *inginja*, *angie*, *inja*, *itch* (recalling the *itji* of the phratries), *itchana*, and the form *anjegoo* which seems to have a double suffix. *Ara*, *yeri*, *aree*, *um*, *ana*, *ula* (as we see by comparing Purula with Burong), *ta*, and the possibly double form *tjuka*, seem to be further examples.

The feminine forms Nalyirri for Thalirri (= Palyeri), Nala for Chula, Ninum for Tjinum, Nana for Tjana or Thama, etc. suggest that prefixes are also to be distinguished. They seem to be *choo*, *joo*, *ja*, *ya*, *n-*, *yun*, *u-*, *ku*, *pu*, *bu*, *nu*, etc. We are however on very uncertain ground here, for the feminine forms may be deliberate creations. Allowance has to be made too for the personal equation of the observer, which is by no means inconsiderable. Possibly this factor, together with ordinary laws of phonetic change, the most elementary principles of which have yet to be established for the Australian languages, will suffice to account for the variations in the names as recorded. Otherwise the words are in most cases reduced to monosyllabic roots from which it seems hopeless to attempt to extract a meaning.

[1] Possibly a prefix also; cf. *Koocheebinga*, *Koorabunna* and their sister names.

These questions of suffixes and prefixes are intimately connected with the very difficult problem of the origin of the classes. The languages of these tribes are at present, if not distinct linguistic stocks, at any rate very far from being mere dialectical variations of a common tongue, for the members of two tribes appear to be mutually unintelligible, unless, contrary to the custom of the American Indians, they are bilingual. But if each tribe added a suffix, and thus adopted into their own language words which, from the general agreement among the class names of this group, seem to have come to them from outside, it is a reasonable hypothesis that the word which they adopted had some meaning for them. Of course we may suppose that the class names were all adopted in the far off time when all spoke a common language. But apart from the difficulty that this presupposes the existence of an eight-class system at that early period, it is clear from the Queensland evidence that class names have been handed on from tribe to tribe, and it is reasonable to suppose this to have been the case with the northern tribes. This conclusion is borne out by the forms of the suffixes, which do not appear to have been developed from one root determinative, as must have been the case if we suppose that the names originated when the language spoken by these tribes was undifferentiated; and by the facts as to the apparent duplication of Koomara, to which allusion has already been made.

The important point about the class, as distinguished from the phratry systems, is the great extent covered by the former. The north-west area of male descent is virtually one from the point of view of class names; two other areas are very large, six are of medium size, three are small, and the remaining one is probably medium.

Although the question of the meaning of the class names is closely bound up with that of their origin, the problem is closely bound up with some of the points discussed in this chapter. The meaning of the eight-class names is connected with the area of origin of the system, and linguistic questions, such as those relating to suffixes, come in. We may therefore briefly discuss at this point the meaning of the class names.

On the whole it may be said that we know the meaning of the class names only in exceptional cases. The Kiabara, Kamilaroi, Annan River, Kuinmurbura, Narrang-ga, and two of the West Australian names can be translated (see Table I.). But with these exceptions we have no certain knowledge of the meaning of the single class names.

Conjectures are of comparatively little value. For in the first place the number of words recorded from any given tribe is as a rule very small, and little or no indication of the pronunciation is given even in the latest works on Australian ethnography. The variations, evidently purely arbitrary and due to the want of training in phonetics, are frequently very considerable. And finally the area over which the names prevail is sufficiently great to give us our choice from half a dozen or more different tribal languages, which combined with the variation in the form of the words, adds very considerably to the probability that there will be found somewhere within the area a word or words bearing a deceptively close resemblance to the class names. How far this is the case may be made clear by one or two instances of chance resemblances between animal names (it seems on the whole probable that if the names are translateable they will turn out to be animal names) in the same or neighbouring tribes. The meaning of Arunta seems to be white cockatoo[1], but we also find a word almost indistinguishable from it in sound—eranta—with the meaning of pelican[2]. Kulbara means emu and koolbirra kangaroo[3]. Malu (= kangaroo), mala (= mouse), and male (= swan) are found in tribes of West Australia, though not of tribes living in immediate proximity one to another[4]. But perhaps the best example is that of Derroein, which, as we have seen, means kangaroo. In addition to durween (young male kangaroo) we find at no great distance the words dirrawong (= iguana) and deerooyn (= whip snake), either of which bears a sufficiently close resemblance to the class name to be accepted as a translation for it in the absence of other competitors[5].

1 Curr, vocab. no. 37.

2 ib. no. 39. Spencer and Gillen give "loud voiced" as the meaning.

3 ib. nos. 34, 40, 49 *a*, 104.

4 Moore, *Vocab.*; Mathew, p. 226.

5 Mathew, p. 232; Curr, nos. 164, 170, 178.

With these facts in mind such suggestions as an attentive study of vocabularies has disclosed are naturally put forward with a full sense of their uncertainty, they are of a purely tentative nature.

For the Koobaroo (var. Obur) of the Goorgilla set I find in the same group the homophone *obur* (gidea tree), which is also a totem of the group of tribes in question[1]. The Wotero of Halifax Bay suggests Wutheru, for which I am unable to find a meaning, unless it be emu, as given by one observer, who however on another occasion gave a different translation. Korkoro in the same set may be the same as korkoren (opossum) of a tribe some 150 miles away[2]. The muri[3] and kubbi of the Kamilaroi and Turribul (?) mean kangaroo and opossum in the latter language, and ibbai means Eaglehawk in Wiraidhuri[4]. The Kamilaroi bundar (= kangaroo) may give us a clue to the meaning of the Dippil Bundar[5]; the Kiabara Bulcoin has a homophone in the Peechera tribe, where it means kangaroo; on the Hastings River it means red wallaby. Balcun however means native bear according to Mathew[6].

If we turn to the eight-class tribes the results are hardly more striking. The Dieri Pultara, Palyara and Upala[7], are homophones of the class names which we have seen as alternative forms; but this very fact makes it certain, or nearly so, that one of the homophones is due to chance coincidence. Bearing in mind that the Arunta alone have the form Bulthara, we may perhaps see in the change undergone by the word in their language the result of attraction, though it must be confessed that the hypothesis is far-fetched in the case of a non-written language. On the other hand it tells against the Palyeri = Palyara equation that the Arunta, who are by far the nearest to the Dieri, use the form Bulthara. The equation Kanunka = Panunga is not backed by any evidence that the p-k change is

[1] ib. no. 143. [2] ib. no. 110.

[3] Elsewhere muri means red kangaroo.

[4] ib. nos. 168, 181, 190; Mathew, *Eaglehawk*, p. 227.

[5] Curr, no. 181.

[6] Mathew, *Eaglehawk*, p. 100; Curr, no. 177.

[7] ib. no. 55.

admissible. Finally three of the four words mentioned seem to be compounded with a suffix; and if this is so it is clearly useless to equate them with words in which this suffix is a component part.

One class name only, Ungilla, is found in the Arunta area itself (and far beyond it, as far as the Gulf of Carpentaria) with the meaning crow[1]. If we may regard the *j* and *k* of the forms jungalla, kungalla, as a prefix, the equation seems justified; otherwise it seems an insuperable difficulty that not the original form of the class name, but the derivative and shortened form is the one to which the equation applies. Our very defective knowledge of the languages of the eight-class tribes makes it possible that when we know more of them other root words may be discovered. At present it can only be said that in very few instances have we either in the four-class or the eight-class areas any warrant for saying that we know the meaning of the class names, much less that we know them to be derived from the names of animals.

One piece of evidence on the subject we need mention only to reject. The Rev. H. Kempe, of the Lutheran Mission among the southern Arunta, has on two occasions stated that the classes in signalling to each other use as their signs the gestures employed to designate animals[2]. On one occasion however he assigns to the Bunanka class the eaglehawk gesture, on another the lizard gesture; the remaining three, which he added only on the second occasion, were ant, wallaby and eaglehawk. It may be noted that the eaglehawk sign is attributed by him to the two classes which would form the main part of the population of a local group; in the second place all four animals are among the totems of the tribe; it seems therefore probable that Mr Kempe has merely confused the sign made to a man of the given kin with a sign which he supposed to be made to a man of a certain class. If he paid little attention to the subject, and especially if on the second occasion he gained his information at a large tribal meeting, the large number of totems would

[1] Roth, *Studies*, p. 50; Curr, nos. 37, 38, 39.

[2] *Halle Verein für Erdkunde*, 1883, p. 52; *Aust. Ass. Adv. Sci.* II, 640.

render it improbable that conflicting evidence would lead him to discover his mistake. If he pursued his enquiries far enough he might, it is true, get more than one sign for a given class; but if he contented himself with asking four men, one of each class, the probability would be that he would get four separate gestures. In any case we have no warrant for arguing that the gesture in any way translates the class name.

# CHAPTER VIII.

## THEORIES OF THE ORIGIN OF CLASSES.

Effect of classes. Dr Durkheim's Theory of Origin. Origin in grouping of totems. Dr Durkheim on origin of eight classes. Herr Cunow's theory of classes.

IN dealing with the origin of the classes it is important to bear in mind that they are undoubtedly later than the phratries. This is clear, not only from the considerations urged on p. 71, but also from the fact that the areas covered by the same classes are in the three most important cases immensely larger than any covered by a phratriac system. We may therefore dismiss at the outset Herr Cunow's theory, which makes the classes the original form of organisation.

To explain the origin of the classes, as of the phratries, two kinds of theories have been put forward, which are in this case also classifiable as reformatory and developmental respectively. The former labour under the same disadvantages, so far as they assume that particular marriages were regarded as immoral or objectionable, as do the similar hypotheses of the origin of phratries.

What is the effect of dividing a phratry into two classes? Firstly and most obviously, to reduce by one half the number of women from whom a man may take his spouse. Secondarily, to put in the forbidden class both his mother's generation and his daughters' generation. It must however not be overlooked that it is the whole class of individuals that are thus put beyond his reach and not those only who stand to him in the relation of daughters in the European sense. Now it is certain that the savage of the present day distinguishes blood relationship from tribal relationship; of this there are plenty of examples in Australia itself[1]. In fact the hypothesis that the introduction of class regulations was due to a desire to prevent the intermarriage of parents and children, more especially of fathers and daughters, the mothers being of course of the same phratries as their sons in the normal tribe, depends for its existence on the assumption that consanguinity was recognised. But it is clearly a clumsy expedient to limit a man's right of choice to the extent we have indicated solely in order to prevent him from marrying his daughter, when the simple prohibition to marry her would, so far as we can see, have been equally effective.

Dr Durkheim has suggested that phratries and classes originated together.

If we start with two exogamous local groups in which the determinant spouse removes, the result is two groups in which both phratries are found, as is evident from the following graphic representation. The two sides represent the local grouping, the letters A and B the phratry names, and m or f male or female; the = denotes marriage, the vertical lines show the children, the brackets show that the person whose symbol is bracketed removes, and the italics that the symbol in question is that of a spouse introduced from without.

| | | | | |
|---|---|---|---|---|
| | mA=*fB* | | mB=fA | |
| [fB] | mB=*fA* | | *fB*=mA | [mB] |
| [fA] | mA=*fB* | | *fA*=mB | [fB] |
| [fB] | mB=*fA* | | *fB*=mA | [fA] |
| | etc. | | | etc. |

We see from this that the alternate generations are in each group A and B, whose spouses are in the same alternation B and A, the male remaining in the group, the female removing in each case, if we assume that the matrilineal kinship is the rule. The permanent members of each group therefore, and in like manner the imported members, are by alternate generations

[1] Roth, *Eth. Stud.* p. 182; Spencer and Gillen, *Nor. Tr.* p. 616; Howitt, p. 262; *J. R. S. N. S. W.* XXXI, 166.

A and B, though of course there is no difference of age actually corresponding to the difference of generation.

By the simple phratry law that A can only marry B, and may marry any B, local group mates are marriageable. The law however which forbids the marriage of phratry mates is on Mr Lang's original theory founded on the prohibition to marry group mates. If we suppose that the primal law or the memory of it continued to work, we have at once a sufficient explanation of the origin of the four-class system. The tribes or nations in which the instinct against intra-group marriage was strong enough to persist as an active principle after the law against intra-phratry marriage had become recognised, may have proceeded to create four classes at a very early stage, while those in whom the feeling for the primal law was less strong adhered to the simple phratry system.

But it is an insuperable objection to this theory that it makes the four-class system originate simultaneously with, or at any rate shortly after, the rise of the phratries. For we cannot suppose that the feeling for the primal law remained dormant for long ages and then suddenly revived. On the other hand we have seen that if the difference in the distribution of the phratry and class names is any guide, a considerable interval must have separated the rise of the one from the rise of the other. Unless therefore it can be shown that some other explanation accounts for the non-coincidence of phratry and class areas, we can hardly accept any explanation of the origin of classes which makes them originate at a period not far removed from the introduction of the phratries.

The fact that a certain number of class names are in character totemic, that is, bear animal names, suggests that the class system may be a development of the totem kins, which in certain cases are grouped within the phratries or otherwise subject to special regulations. In the Urabunna the choice of a man of one totem is said to be limited to women of the right status in a single totem of the opposite phratry. Among the similarly organised Yandairunga the limitation is to certain totems, and Dr Howitt gives other examples of the same order. In the Kongulu tribe these totemic classes seem to have been known by special names. In the Wotjoballuk tribe there are sub-totems, grouped with certain totems, which again seem to be collected into aggregates intermediate between the phratry and the simple totem kin. But it is difficult to see why, if the classes have arisen out of such organisations, there should be found over the great part of Australia four, and only four, classes from which the eight have obviously developed. In any case we have no parallel in these modifications to the alternate generations of the class system.

These find an analogue, according to an old report, not subsequently confirmed, in the Wailwun tribe, where, however, it is supplementary to the classes. We are told that there are four totems in this tribe, though this does not agree with other reports, and that they are found in both phratries indiscriminately. A woman's children do not take her totem, nor, apparently, the totem of her brother, who belongs to a different kin, but are of the remaining two totems according to their sex[1]. From this it follows that the totems alternate, precisely as do the classes; the difference in the arrangement consists in the distinction of totem falling to males and females, which has no analogue in the class system. But such arrangements, even if we may take them as established facts, are clearly of secondary origin, and can hardly give a clue to the origin of the classes.

There is an important difference between the four-class and eight-class organisations in respect of the totem kins. In the former systems the kins are almost invariably divided between the phratries; but within them they do not belong to either of the classes, though certain classes claim them[2]; but on the contrary, of necessity are divided between them. In the eight-class tribes this seems to be the case in some tribes also; in others, like the Arunta, abnormalities of development cause the totems to fall in both phratries. But in the Mara, the Mayoo, and the Warramunga[3] they fall, or are stated to fall, in the first case into groups according to the four classes, in the other cases according to the "couples," i.e. the two classes which stand in

[1] *J. A. I.* VII, 249, cf. *J. R. S. N. S. W.* XXXI, 172.

[2] Howitt, p. 110.

[3] *Nor. Tr.* p. 167; *Proc. R. G. S. Qu.* XVI, 70; *J.R.S.N.S.W.* XXX, 111, 112.

the relation of parent and child (the son of Panunga is Appungerta, his son is again Panunga, and so for the other pairs). This suggests that totemism has something to do with the division of the four classes into eight, as was pointed out by Dr Durkheim in 1905[1]. His argument is that as long as descent was in the female line, the rule was that a man could not marry a woman of his mother's totem. When the change to male descent took place, the mother's totem, as we see by actual examples[2], did not lose the respect which it formerly enjoyed ; there is in more than one tribe a tabu of the mother's as well as of the father's totem. That being so, it is natural to suppose that the new marriage organisation according to male descent might be modified to take account of this fact. By dividing the classes and arranging that one member of a couple should be debarred not only from intermarrying with the class of his mother, for which the four-class system also provides, but also from intermarrying with the second member of the same couple too, this result was attained, in the view of Dr Durkheim.

It remains however to be established that this segregation of totems is actually found in the tribes in question. For the Warramunga Spencer and Gillen distinctly state[3] that the arrangement is dichotomous, in which case the alleged result would not be brought about. The Anula and Mara are exceptional tribes with direct male descent; it is hardly likely that the eight-class system spread from them. The Mayoo have not yet been reported on by an expert. Finally some of the tribes have not even the dichotomous arrangement of totems but distribute them in both phratries. The basis of the hypothesis, therefore, is hardly established.

Singularly enough, Dr Durkheim[4] expresses his adherence to a previous theory of his own as to the method of effecting the change from female to male descent in four-class tribes. This he supposes to have been done by transferring one of the two classes from each phratry to the opposite one; and in the former discussion (*Année Soc.* V, 82 sq.) he showed that this

[1] *Ann. Soc.* VIII, 118.

[2] Spencer and Gillen, *Nor. Tr.* p. 166.

[3] *Nor. Tr.* p. 163.

[4] p. 142.

procedure would result in scattering the totems through both phratries, as we find them to be in the case of the Arunta. It is therefore singular to find that he adheres to this theory when his new hypothesis demands that the totems, so far from being more widely distributed, should be actually confined to the members of one couple. Beyond the Urabunna custom in intertribal marriages, however, which is hardly decisive evidence, there does not appear to be any proof that the transference from one phratry to the other ever took place.

The further support claimed by Dr Durkheim for his hypothesis from the alleged male descent of the totem in tribes where female descent of the class names prevails, rests on too uncertain a basis to make it necessary to deal with it at length; some criticism of the evidence will be found elsewhere.

We have seen above that the Dieri rule is precisely parallel to that of the eight-class tribes in practice; it is however expressed, not by a class system, but by enacting that people standing in a certain degree of kinship or consanguinity shall marry. If Dr Durkheim's theory of the origin of the eight-class system is correct, it should also apply to the Dieri. Now the rule that a man must marry his maternal great-uncle's daughter clearly prevents intermarriage with one of the mother's totem; but this cannot be the object of the rule, for it is prevented already by the phratry system. Dr Durkheim's theory therefore finds no support in the Dieri rule.

On the other hand, unless the totems have been scattered through the phratries since the southern Arunta divided their classes, Dr Durkheim will have difficulty in explaining why a tribe where the totem does not concern marriage at all has found it necessary to split the classes; and that though the child does not take its totem from mother or father.

Herr Cunow has advanced the view that the classes correspond to distinctions of age; but he took as his basis, not the differentia of elder and younger, but the distinction made by the initiation customs, which divide the community, in his view, into three strata—young, adult and old. Into the difficulties created by this theory we need not here enter. Suffice it to say that the theory depends on the supposition that an age-grade had to marry within itself. Now the age-grade is not a fixed body, but is continually changing its personnel; not only so, but it is difficult to see how marriage could take place, given the initiation ceremonies, in any other way; unions of "old men" with adult women apart, which are not, in fact, prohibited, so far as is known, the only marriages possible are those within the adult grade. Although father and son can rarely belong to the adult grade simultaneously, mother and daughter can readily do so. If not, these grades are clearly generation classes, and what Herr Cunow really takes as the basis of his theory is the generation in each family. This can readily be shown by a consideration of the kinship terms.

# CHAPTER IX.

## KINSHIP TERMS.

Descriptive and classificatory systems. Kinship terms of Wathi-Wathi, Ngerikudi-speaking people and Arunta. Essential features. Urabunna. Dieri. Distinction of elder and younger.

SOME classless two-phratry tribes observe in practice the same rules as the four and eight class tribes when they are deciding what marriages are permissible. The Dieri and Narrangga follow the eight-class rule; the position of the Urabunna is somewhat uncertain owing to the obscurity of our authorities, which again is probably due to their lack of intimate acquaintance with the tribe; and the Wolgal, Ngarrego and Murring have the simple four-class rule that a man marries his mother's brother's daughter.

We have seen in an earlier chapter that kinship and consanguinity are distinct in their nature, though among civilised peoples they are not in practice distinguishable. In the lower stages of culture it is otherwise, as will be shown in detail below. Corresponding to this distinction of consanguinity and kinship but not parallel to it we have two ways of expressing these relationships—the descriptive and the classificatory. The terminology of the former system is based on the principle of reckoning the relationship of two people by the total number of steps between them and the nearest lineal ancestor of both. The latter does not concern itself with descent at all but expresses the status of the individual as a member of a group of persons. Thus, to take a single example, in a typical Australian tribe the word applied by a child to its father is not used of him alone but of all the other males on the same level of a generation provided they belong to the same phratry; to the other half of the generation is applied the term usually translated "mother's brother."

Unfortunately but few Australian lists of kinship terms have been drawn up, and the anomalous tribes like the Kurnai have absorbed a large share of attention. It is however possible to give tables for the three classes of tribes with which we have been in the main concerned. Those given are in use among the Wathi-Wathi of Victoria, the Ngerikudi-speaking people of North Queensland and the Arunta[1].

*Wathi-Wathi Tribe: two-phratry.*

| *Phratry A* | | *Phratry B* | | Generation |
|---|---|---|---|---|
| | *Naponui* (mother's father) *Miimui* (father's mother) | | *Kokonui* (mother's mother) *Matui* (father's father) | I |
| *Mamui* (father) *Niingui* (father's sister = *Nalundui*, wife's mother) | | *Kukui* (mother) *Gunui* (mother's brother = *Nguthanguthu* wife's father) | | II |
| | *Malunui* (father's sister's son) *Neripui* (father's sister's daughter = wife) | | EGO *Wawi*, *mamui* (elder brother, sister) *Tatui*, *minukui* (younger do.) | III |
| *Waipui* (son, daughter) | | *Ngipui* (sister's son) ? (sister's dau. = *Boikathui*, son's wife) | | IV |
| | *Naponui* (daughter's son) *Miimui* (sister's son's son) | | *Kokonui* (sister's daughter's son) *Matui* (son's son) | V |

[1] *J. A. I.* XIV, 354; *N. Queensl. Eth. Bull.* VI, 6; Spencer and Gillen, *Northern Tribes*, p. 90.

*Ngerikudi: Four-class.*

| *Phratry A: Class a* | *Class $a_1$* | *Phratry B: Class b* | *Class $b_1$* | Generation |
|---|---|---|---|---|
| | *Daida* (mother's father)<br>*Baida* (father's mother) | | *Mite* (mother's mother)<br>*Laeta* (father's father) | I |
| *Naider* (father)<br>*Wiata* (father's brother)<br>*Niata* (elder sister)<br>*Wiata* (younger do.) | | *Naibeguta* (mother)<br>*Miata* (brother)<br>*Goete* (elder sister)<br>*Datu* (younger do.) | | II |
| | *Danuma* (wife = mo. bro. dau.)<br>*Lanti ngenuma* (sister's husband = mo. bro. son) | | EGO<br>*Maneinga* (elder brother)<br>*Goete* (elder sister)<br>*Otro* (younger brother or sister) | III |
| *Yuta* (son or daughter) | | ? (sister's son or daughter)<br>*Yamaanta* (dau.'s husband) | | IV |
| | *Yudanta* (daughter's child) | | *Yuunta* (son's child) | V |

So far as deficiencies in our information would allow, these tables have been drawn up on corresponding lines, and the first point which strikes us is the great similarity between the three tables, in spite of the apparent wide divergence in the kinship organisation of the tribes. To facilitate comparison the Wathi-Wathi terms have been arranged, not only according to the system in use in the tribe, but in such a way as to show how the terms would be arranged under the four-class system.

In the Wathi-Wathi system, we observe that in each generation there are two groups of males and two of females,

*Arunta: Eight-class.*

| *Panunga* | *Uknaria* | *Bulthara* | *Appungerta* | *Purula* | *Ungalla* | *Kumara* | *Umbitchana* | Generation |
|---|---|---|---|---|---|---|---|---|
| | | *Ipmunna* (mother's mother, wife's mother's father) | *Arunga* (father's father) | | | *Tjimmia* (mother's father) | *Aperla* (father's mother) | I |
| *Oknia* (father) *Uwinna* (father's sisters) | *Mura* (wife's mother, wife's mother's brothers) | | | *Mia* (mother, mother's sister) *Gammona* (mother's brother) | *Ikuntera* (wife's father) | | | II |
| | | *Ipmunna* (father's sister's daughter's husband, son's wife's mother) | EGO *Okilia* (elder brothers) *Ungaraitcha* (elder sisters) *Itia* (younger brothers and sisters) | | | *Unkulla* (father's sister's sons) | *Unawa* (wife, wife's sisters) *Umbirna* (wife's brother = sister's husband) | III |
| *Allira* (children, brother's children) | | | | *Gammona* (son's wife) | *Umba* (sister's children) | | | IV |
| | | | *Arunga* (son's son) | | | *Tjimmia* (daughter's child) | | V |

corresponding to the two-phratry system, which are distinguished by names differing for each generation. Precisely the same arrangement is found in the four-class tribe. The four-class are therefore simply a systematisation of the terms of kinship in use under the two-phratry system.

Comparing now the eight-class with the four-class system, we do not see at a glance the essential principle of the former. The clue is given by the fact that classes I and IV, II and III in phratry A, I and II, III and IV in phratry B, are what we have termed a couple, that is to say stand in the relation of parent and child alternately. Marriage being between classes of corresponding numbers, it follows that Kumara-Bulthara and Appungerta-Umbitchana are the maternal and paternal grandparents of the man EGO. The grandparents of his wife are in the same classes but with reversal as regards the sex. Bulthara is the cousin of Appungerta, Kumara of Umbitchana and so on. We see therefore that, just as among the Dieri, a man may not marry his cousin, but must marry his second cousin, to use ordinary terms, which in this case are not misleading.

Looking now at the Ngerikudi system, we see that elder and younger sisters are distinguished in the generations of EGO and his parents. Possibly they are the eight-class tribe of Queensland to which Dr Howitt alludes. If not, we have in them a tribe one stage earlier than the southern Arunta, who have their four classes divided but as yet without any corresponding names.

The Dieri rule is that of the eight-class tribes. The person designated as the proper spouse for a male is his mother's mother's brother's daughter's daughter, in other words, the grandchildren of brother and sister intermarry. This, as we have already seen, is precisely the effect of the eight-class rules. We are therefore confronted with three possibilities. Either the Dieri regulations are aberrant or they have introduced these rules under the influence of the neighbouring eight-class system; or the eight-class organisation is a systematisation of the Dieri rule, adopted perhaps to facilitate the determination of marriageableness or otherwise in the case of persons residing at some distance from each other and therefore less likely to be acquainted with genealogical niceties than the members of a small community. Now if the second of these hypotheses is correct, it is by no means clear why the Dieri, having in view the attainment of the object of the eight-class system, did not simply adopt it; for this we can find no reason; and it is clearly more reasonable on other grounds to suppose that these regulations are of independent origin. But we know the eight-class rule to have arisen from a division within a generation, which the Dieri rule is not. Therefore the latter must be sporadic.

The same is probably true of the Urabunna, but here our information is very scanty and the precise working of the rules is far from clear. What happens is that an elder brother (A) of a woman (B) marries an elder sister (D) of a man (C); the daughter of this elder sister (D) is the proper mate for the son of the younger sister (B) of her husband; this younger sister's husband is the younger brother, C. Now the term elder brother, elder sister, does not seem to refer to age; the rule appears to be—once an elder brother, always an elder brother from generation to generation.

We learn from Spencer and Gillen, that all the women of a generation in the one phratry, and presumably within the right totem only, are to a man either *nupa* (= marriageable) or *apillia*. In the case given by Dr Howitt the younger sister is *nupa* to the younger brother, the elder to the elder brother; but we do not learn how elder and younger are distinguished, if it is not by descent. Apparently it cannot be by descent, however; for we find that the son of the younger brother and sister marries the daughter of the elder brother and sister. As to what would happen if the younger brother and sister have a daughter, the elder a son, we have no information; but apparently they cannot marry. Such a daughter must find the son of two people who stand to her father and mother as they stood to A and D.

From this example it is clear that the boundaries of the *nupa* and *apillia* groups are not fixed in a given group of women; it is not possible to divide the women and the men into elder brothers and sisters on the one hand, younger brothers and sisters on the other. But if this is the case, we are quite in the dark as to the meaning of the marriage regulations.

One thing however seems certain; viz., that the Urabunna regulations do not give the same result as the four-class regulations. With them the division is within the generation. There is no class of women, who, with their descendants, are the normal spouses of a class of men, with their descendants. That being so, the Urabunna case can hardly throw light on the genesis of the four-class system.

Among the Urabunna, however, like the Wathi-Wathi, we find the rule that a man must marry in his own generation; and this is *primâ facie* the meaning of the four-class rule. It is true that the origin of the eight-class rule was not what its *primâ facie* meaning suggests, viz., the desire to prevent the marriage of cousins, for we know that it originated in the distinction between elder and younger sisters. But no similar theory appears to fit the case of the four-class tribes. No division within the generation could possibly produce an alternation of generations.

The Red Indians have in many cases different names for the elder and younger sister; the Hausa impose on persons standing in these relations certain prohibitions and avoidances, which are not the same for both elder and younger; in Australia a man may speak freely to his elder sisters in blood, but only at a distance to his tribal *ungaraitcha*. To his younger sisters, blood and tribal, he may not speak save at such a distance that his features are indistinguishable. In many parts the elder brother has special rights with regard to the younger, and many similar customs might be quoted[1].

The question why marriage within the generation—the rule of four-class and two-phratry tribes alike—should have come into existence is a complicated one and involves that of the origin of kinship terms. If we take a crucial case of kinship terminology, we find that a child applies the same term to its actual mother as to all the women whom its father might have married, to its potential mothers in fact. If therefore we have to choose between the gradual extension of the terms from the single family to the group or their original application to a group, this instance seems decisive in favour of the latter theory.

[1] Morgan, in *Smithsonian Contr.* vol. XVII; *Globus*, LXIX, 3; *Nat. Tribes*, pp. 88—9.

Now if marriage was originally not "group" but individual, a question to be fully discussed in later chapters, we can hardly doubt that parent-child marriage was forbidden or perhaps instinctively avoided. But this would be equivalent to prohibiting marriage with one of a number of men or women embraced under a common kinship term. In the lower culture generally and especially among the Australians there is a tendency to follow things out to their logical conclusions. If this were done in the present case, the result would be to extend the prohibition to all the persons embraced under the kinship term.

In any case the natural tendency in a small group would be to marry within the generation, and this might readily become crystallised in the kinship terms.

The eight-class system, as we have seen, resulted from the distinction between elder and younger sister. What is the meaning of this and what analogies do we find to it?

Widely extended also are the systems of age-grades. In all parts of the world the men, and sometimes the women, are or have been divided into associations, to which reference was made in Chapter I, which begin by being co-extensive with the tribe for all practical purposes, since all pass through the initiation ceremonies. The various initiation ceremonies during what may be termed the involuntary stage of these associations, no less than in their later form of secret societies, determine the rights and duties of the individuals who undergo them. The period at which they take place is determined, broadly speaking, by the age of the individual. It is therefore clear that for the peoples in the lower stage of culture considerations of age are of the highest importance.

We find that in practice the elder brother has much authority, both over the younger brother and the sister. In Victoria he decides whom they are to marry. As we have seen in the tables of terms, the Wathi-Wathi man distinguishes both elder and younger of either sex by special terms, which points to their having special rights or duties[1].

If therefore we cannot see why primitive man should have

[1] For lists of tribes where this distinction is found see Mathew, *Eaglehawk*, p. 223—4.

enacted that the elder rather than the younger, or the daughter of the elder rather than the daughter of the younger, should be preferred, it is at any rate of a piece with his other customs.

From the terms of kinship tabulated above various conclusions have been drawn. It will be seen that a man applies to all the women in the other phratry on the level of his generation the same term as he applies to his actual wife. On this basis it has been argued that at one time all the men in one phratry were united in marriage with all the women in the other within the limits of the generation. Before this again a stage of absolute promiscuity is supposed to have existed. This alternative explanation of the kinship organisations demands to be considered.

# CHAPTER X.

## TYPES OF SEXUAL UNIONS.

Terminology of Sociology. Marriage. Classification of Types. Hypothetical and existing forms.

STUDENTS of the sociology of white races enjoy conspicuous advantages over those who devote themselves to the investigation of the organisation of races in the lower stages of culture. In the first place they deal with conditions and forms with which they are personally familiar; and this familiarity is shared by those who form the audience, or the reading public, of these investigators, who may thus count on making themselves understood. Even should they find the already existing terminology insufficient, the knowledge of the phenomena enables them to introduce suitable modifications or innovations without fear of causing misunderstanding. It is true that terminology is often loose, but it exists and can be made to express what is meant.

The student of primitive sociology, on the other hand, is called upon to digest the reports of other observers, who have not always understood the conditions which they describe, who have failed to define to themselves what they are endeavouring to make clear to others, and who make use of a terminology created for an entirely different set of conditions, as if exact definition and care in the use of terms were the last and not the first duty of the observer when he frames his report.

Thus, to take a concrete example, there is not much danger that a writer who discusses the question of marriage in civilised communities will deal with one form of union of the sexes, while his readers may imagine that he is dealing with another form. For marriage is the form of sexual union recognised by the law of the land, and its legal sanction distinguishes it from all other forms of sexual union, however permanent they may be, and however short may be the period before the marriage is dissolved by an appeal to the courts of law. In fact in civilised communities the fulfilment of legal forms and ceremonies constitutes marriage, whatever might be said of a union sanctioned by legal forms but unaccompanied by the cohabitation of the parties. When, however, we are dealing with a people ruled by custom and not by law, the case is far different. The force of custom may and usually does in such cases far exceed the force of law in civilised communities. In the lower stages of culture there is far more reluctance to overstep the traditional lines of behaviour than is felt by the ordinary member of a European state, and this though there are penalties in the latter which do not necessarily exist in the former case. But law, in the sense of a rule of conduct, promulgated by a legislator and enforced by penalties inflicted by law courts and carried out by the agents of the state, does not necessarily exist, and, at most, exists only in a very inchoate state. If therefore we read of marriage among such a people, we are left in complete uncertainty whether it is a union corresponding to marriage in civilised lands, or whether it belongs to a different category. The difficulty of the case lies partly in the inability of the observer to distinguish *de jure* from *de facto* unions, partly in the fact that one may be transformed into the other, and no ceremony of any sort mark the change. An Australian may, for example, have a wife who is recognised as his by tribal custom and tradition; if she is abducted the aggrieved husband may vindicate his rights but will not necessarily be supported by even his own kin, and will certainly not find anything to correspond to the tribunal before which an Englishman would sue for the restitution of conjugal rights. If the aggrieved husband proves the weaker, he necessarily abandons his wife, and she becomes *ipso facto* the wife of the aggressor; divorce is in fact pronounced by the issue of an ordeal by combat. So far the matter is clear to the observer.

But if the aggrieved husband take no steps to vindicate his rights, the woman will equally pass to the aggressor, and in this case there will be no customary ceremonial to mark for the benefit of the observer the exact moment of the transition from a marriage, recognised by public opinion, or tribal custom, with the first husband A to the same kind of union with B.

Again, even where no second mate intervenes to complicate the question, the observer may be confronted with delicate problems ; at what point, for example, does a mere liaison pass into something worthy of the name of marriage? What is the status of a union in which the parties are more or less permanently associated, but which confers no rights as against aggressors? If by native custom the union is not of such a nature as to confer on the male party to it any rights over the female, such as the liberty to chastise or punish without fear of the intervention of the woman's kin, are we to regard the tie as equivalent to marriage if only it is permanent? At what point does mere cohabitation pass into marriage?

All these are questions which have to be debated and decided before we are in possession of a suitable terminology for dealing with the unions of the sexes in the lower stages of culture. But they are commonly neglected in controversies as to the origin and history of human marriage.

We have seen above that in a European community we mean by marriage a union between two persons of opposite sexes, entered into with due legal formalities, and not dissoluble simply at the will of either or both the parties concerned. When we go further afield the connotation of the term is extended to embrace (1) polygyny, in which one male is associated with two or more females, (2) polyandry, in which one female is similarly associated with more than one male, and (3) the condition which I propose to term polygamy, in which both these conditions are found. In all these cases the union is properly termed marriage, in so far as it cannot be entered upon without due formalities nor be dissolved without the concurrence of the authority upon the carrying out of whose conditions in the preliminary steps the union depends for its marriage-character.

When however we come to the so-called group marriage, using the term in its original sense of limited promiscuity, we are dealing with an entirely different state of things, and it is difficult to see any justification for the use of the term marriage in this connection at all. By group marriage is meant a condition only removed from absolute promiscuity by the existence of age-classes or of two or more exogamous classes in the community; it demands no special ceremonies prior to the individual union[1], it permits this union to be dissolved at will, and it consequently confers no rights on either of the parties to it, other than perhaps the right to the produce, or some of the produce, of each other's labour.

If the confusion did not extend beyond the terminology, the advance of knowledge would perhaps be but little impeded; but experience shows that confusion in terminology is apt to go hand in hand with confusion in ideas. As will be shown later, this seems to be particularly true of investigations into the history of marriage and sexual relationships. It seems desirable therefore to clear the way by classifying the ideas with which we have to deal, and by defining the terms corresponding to them.

Before classifying the various forms of sexual relationships, it may be well to say a few words on the definition of marriage in general. Dr Westermarck has defined it from the point of view of natural history as a more or less durable connection between male and female, lasting beyond the mere act of propagation till after the birth of the offspring.

It may not be possible to propose a better definition from the point of view selected by Dr Westermarck, which is certainly the one from which anthropology must regard sexual relationships. At the same time it is not entirely free from objection. In the first place we are employing the word marriage in a sense which has but little in common with its ordinarily accepted meaning. Suppose, for example, we are dealing with marriage in Europe, it is confusing to be compelled by our definition to regard as a marriage the *faux ménage*, not to speak of the not uncommon fairly permanent unions in which there is no common residence. Such monogamous relationships may be, technically speaking, marriages, in Dr Westermarck's sense, but

[1] The *pirrauru* union is preceded by a ceremony, but this is no proof that primitive group marriage, if it existed, was contracted in the same way.

it seems desirable to make use of some other term for them and reserve marriage for the unions sanctioned by legal forms. Or take the union of two people, each of whom has prior matrimonial engagements. Such a union may, as the records of the divorce court show, be anything but impermanent; but it does not make for clearness to call such an union marriage. Let us take a third example—a New Hebridean girl purchased, or in Upa stolen, for the use of the young men, who, of course, reside in their club-house. If any of the bachelors there resident chooses to recognise her children, they are regarded as his children; if not, they are supported by the whole of the residents in the club-house. How are we to classify the position of the mother of these children? The union is obviously fairly permanent, although some of the group enter into sexual relationships of an ordinary type and join the ranks of the married men, and others enter the club-house from the ranks of those hitherto shut out from the enjoyment of the privileges of the adult unmarried male. But the relationship established with the whole body of unmarried men and indistinguishable, so far as definition goes, from polyandry, hardly seems to be a permanent union of the type which Dr Westermarck had in mind when he framed his definition, much less a marriage in any accepted sense of the term.

For Dr Westermarck's general term marriage it would be well to substitute *gamé* or gamic union, to express all kinds of sexual relationships other than temporary ones. As sub-heads under this we have:

(1) Marriage, a union recognised by law or custom, which imposes duties and confers rights on one, both, or all the parties to it.

(2) Free union, a relationship not recognised by the community as conferring rights, but at the same time not punished and not necessarily regarded as immoral. Temporary unions we may classify as (*a*) promiscuity, where marriage does not exist or is temporarily in abeyance: (*b*) free love, the relationships of the unmarried: (*c* i.) temporary polyandry or polygyny of married people, where the unions are limited and recognised by custom: (*c* ii.) marital licence where the husband is complai-

sant in the face of public opinion: (*c* iii.) adultery where neither the husband nor public opinion permits them.

(3) Liaison, a union in which one or both parties have other ties, which renders them liable to punishment, or to some kind of atonement.

Ten various possible forms of sexual relationship actually found or assumed to have existed may now be classified.

## A. PROMISCUITY.

I. Unregulated Promiscuity. (*a*) Primary unregulated promiscuity is the hypothetical state assumed by Morgan and others to be the primitive state of mankind. It may be noted that promiscuity *de jure*, which is all that is implied by Morgan's hypothesis, is not necessarily also *de facto* promiscuity. Unless it be assumed that jealousy was absent at this stage, it is clear that free unions must have been the rule rather than the exception. But if this be so, the only distinction between Morgan's promiscuity and the ordinary state of things in an Australian tribe is constituted, intermarrying rules apart, by the fact that the Australian husband is at liberty to reclaim his wife, if he can, without fear of blood feud if perchance he slays his successor in the affections, or perhaps rather in the possession, of his wife, whereas in Morgan's primitive stage might was right and the abductor was on an equal footing with his predecessor and successor. (*b*) Secondary unregulated promiscuity is distinguished from primary promiscuity by the co-existence of other forms of sexual relations. It may temporarily supersede these as in Australia; or it may take their place, as among the Nairs.

II. Regulated Promiscuity. This again falls into (*a*) primary regulated promiscuity, the hypothetical stage postulated for Australia before the introduction of individual marriage; and (*b*) secondary regulated promiscuity, which is found in certain tribes as an exceptional practice. With this custom I deal in greater detail below.

## B. MARRIAGE.

III, Polygamy. This state is constituted by the union of several men with several women. It may be distinguished, as before, into primary and secondary polygamy. We may further distinguish (*a*) simple and (*β*) adelphic polygamy; and the latter may be (i) unilateral or (ii) bilateral, according as either the males or females, or both males and females, are brothers and sisters. A further sub-division is constituted by the relations of the groups of males or females, or both, within themselves. I distinguish these unions by the names of dissimilar (M.) and dissimilar (F.) according as one husband or one wife has a position superior to the others[1].

IV, Polyandric and V. polygynic unions fall into the same divisions, save that they are naturally always unilateral. As a designation for the hypothetical stage postulated by Mr Atkinson in *Primal Law*, we may take "patriarchal polygyny," meaning thereby the state in which (*a*) in the earlier stage all the females of the horde[2] are *ipso facto* mates of the one adult male of the horde; or (*b*) in the second stage all females born in the horde are equally allotted to him.

Finally we have VI, monogamy.

To the three forms of marriage we can apply the determinants "regulated" and "unregulated," "temporary[3]," "permanent," as in the case of promiscuity.

We have further two well-marked types of marriage and a mixed form in which (*a*) the husband goes to live with the wife; (*b*) he lives with the wife for a time and then removes to his own village or tribe; and (*c*) the wife removes to the husband. For the first of these Maclennan has proposed the name *beena* marriage; Robertson Smith has proposed to call the third type *ba'al* marriage, and to include both *beena* and *mot'a* marriages under the general name of *ṣadīca.* This terminology is unnecessarily obscure and has the further disadvantage of con-

[1] Dissimilar polygamy is, in respect of the inferior spouses, hardly to be distinguished from promiscuity, save that the number of them is limited. But in Australia the lending of *pirraurus* sweeps away even this distinction.

[2] He says family, or Cyclopean family. Harem in fact is the idea.

[3] i.e. not life-long.

noting the domination or subjection of the husband, a feature not necessarily bound up with residence. I therefore propose to term the three types matrilocal, removal, and patrilocal marriages. I suggest compounds of *pater* and *mater*, not as being specially appropriate, but as being parallel to matrilineal and patrilineal, denoting descent in the female and male lines respectively.

For the somewhat complicated relationships of *potestas* in the family I propose two main divisions, (*a*) patri-potestal, (*b*) matri-potestal; the latter may be further subdivided according as the authority is in the hands (1) of the actual mother, (2) of the maternal uncles, (3) of the mother's relatives in general, and so on.

# CHAPTER XI.

## GROUP MARRIAGE AND MORGAN'S THEORIES.

Passage from Promiscuity. Reformatory Movements. Incest. Relative harmfulness of such unions. Natural aversion. Australian facts.

THE arguments for group marriage in Australia are of two kinds—(1) from the terms of relationship, that is to say of a mixed philological and sociological character, and (2) from the customs of the Australian tribes.

The argument from the terms of relationship is so intimately connected with the theories of Lewis Morgan that it may be well to give a brief critical survey of Morgan's hypotheses. I therefore begin the treatment of this part of the subject by a statement of Morgan's views on the general question of the origin and development of human marriage.

As a result of his enquiries into terms of relationships, mainly in North America and Asia, Morgan drew up a scheme of fifteen stages, through which he believed the sexual relations of human beings had passed in the interval between utter savagery and the civilised family. We are only concerned with the earlier portion of his scheme. It is not even necessary to discuss that in all its details. Morgan's first eight (properly five) stages are:

I. Promiscuous Intercourse.

II. Intermarriage or Cohabitation of Brothers and Sisters.

III. The Communal Family (First stage of the Family).

IV. The Hawaiian Custom of Punalua[1], giving the Malayan Form of the Classificatory System[2].

[1] This is not really material.

[2] Properly speaking these are not stages in the same sense as the other forms.

V. The Tribal Organisation, i.e. totemic exogamy plus promiscuity, giving the Turanian and Ganowanian System[1].

VI. Monogamy.

The objections to this theory or group of theories are numerous, and it will not be necessary to consider them all here. Were it not that no one has since Morgan's day attempted to trace in detail the course of evolution from promiscuity to monogamy, it would be almost superfluous to discuss the theories of a work on primitive sociology dating back nearly thirty years.

With some points Morgan has failed to deal in a way that commends itself to us in the light of knowledge accumulated since his day; with others he has not attempted to deal, apparently from a want of perception of their importance.

First and foremost among the points with which Morgan has failed to deal is that of the constitution of the primitive group. Was it composed of parents and children only or were more than two generations represented? If the former, why were the children expelled? if the latter, how are brother and sister marriages introduced, when *ex hypothesi* the father of any given child was unknown and may have been any adult male? If Morgan and his supporters evade this difficulty by defining brother and sister as children of the same mother, they are met by the obvious objection that no revolution in a promiscuous group would result in the marriage of children of the same mother. *Ex hypothesi* there were several child-bearing women in the group, and their children, if a reform were introduced prohibiting marriage outside one's own generation, would intermarry; but the children of these women are, on the definition adopted, not brothers and sisters.

If brother and sister does not mean children of the same mother, what does it mean?

By what process are these names supposed to have come into existence in a promiscuous group? If brother in this sense is taken to imply common parentage, the name must clearly denote the relation between two males because, although a whole group of men had access to the mother, the male parent

[1] See note 2 on previous page.

was or may have been the same person in each case, and this whether the mother was the same or not. Now, quite apart from the fact that primitive man was unlikely to have evolved a term for such an indefinite relationship, except in so far as it involved rights or duties, it is obvious that great complications would arise which would in practice make the nomenclature unworkable. For to call two boys brothers because they have the same group of men as possible fathers is only practicable in a society which has already evolved a system of age grades, and has established restrictions on intercourse between different generations, to use a somewhat indefinite term. For it is clear that in a state of promiscuity the class of adults is continually being recruited and that the boy passes at puberty, in so far as restrictions in the nature of initiation ceremonies are not imposed, from the class of sons to that of fathers. In other words, if a group consists of $M_1$ $M_2$ $M_3$ $M_4$, and they have male children of all ages $N_1$ $N_2$ $N_3$ $N_4$, as soon as $N_1$ reaches puberty he becomes a possible father of the children $O_1$ $O_2$ $O_3$ $O_4$, who differ in age from $N_4$ only by a few years at most and reckon as his brothers. But this means that $N_1$ is the son of $M_1$, for example, but at the same time the father of $O_1$, who is likewise the son of $M_1$; in the same way $O_1$ is the brother of $N_4$, who is the brother of $N_1$; but $O_1$ is not the brother of $N_1$. The extraordinary complexity of the relations that would arise is at once obvious, and it seems clear that relationship terms could never come into existence under such circumstances unless they implied something beyond mere relationship and denoted rights and duties[1]. But if they denoted rights and duties, these must have preceded the relationship term, which consequently need not be held to apply to kinship in any proper sense of the term.

It is clear that the same difficulties apply when we try to work out the development on the hypothesis that a group of mothers existed. We are therefore reduced to the supposition that the term brother denoted originally a person born within a given period of time, and that this period was the same for

[1] We find that in practice change of age grade, i.e. of relationship term, does exist; a clearer proof could not be given that the term of relationship has nothing to do with descent.

whole sections of the community; in other words that the name brother was given to all males born between, let us say, B.C. 10,000 and B.C. 9,990. This is of course equivalent to the establishment of age grades and is in itself not unthinkable; age grades are of course perfectly well known among primitive peoples; but the establishment of age grades implies a degree of social organisation; and, what is more important, this hypothesis makes the term brother quite meaningless as a kinship term; for at the present day a common term of address for members of an age grade does not imply any degree of consanguinity, and unless it be proved that age grades are a product of the period of "group marriage" it cannot be argued that they ever did imply kinship.

It is sufficiently clear from these examples that Morgan entirely failed to work out the process by which the transition from pure to regulated promiscuity came about. But if the process is uncertain the causes are equally obscure. In Mr Morgan's view, or at any rate in one of the theories on which he accounted for the change, it was due to "movements which resulted in unconscious reformation"; these movements were, he supposes, worked out by natural selection. These words, it is true, apply primarily to the origin of the "tribal" or "gentile" organisation, as Mr Morgan terms totemism, but they probably apply to the original passage from promiscuity to "communal marriage," and I propose to examine how far such a theory has any solid basis.

Natural selection is a blessed phrase, but in the present case it is difficult to see in what way it is supposed to act. The variation postulated by Mr Morgan as a basis for the operation of natural selection is one of ideas, not physical or mental powers. Now under ordinary circumstances we mean by natural selection the weeding out of the unfit by reason of inferiorities, physical or psychical, which handicap them in the struggle for existence. But it cannot be said that the tendency to marry or practice of marrying outside one's own generation is such a handicap to the parents. How far is it injurious to the children of such unions? Or rather, how far have children who are the offspring of brothers and sisters or of cousins a better chance of surviving than the offspring of unions between relatives of different generations?

It is at the outset clear that savages are not in the habit of taking account of such matters. Even if it were otherwise, it is not clear how far they would have data as to the varying results of unions of near kin. For though on this question, so far as the genus homo is concerned, we have very few data on which to go, such data as we have hardly bear out his view. Modern statistics relate almost exclusively to the intermarriage of cousins, and apply, not to primitive tribes, such as those with which, *ex hypothesi*, Mr Morgan is dealing, but to more or less civilised and sophisticated peoples, among whom the struggle for existence is less keen owing to the advance of knowledge and the progress of invention, and among whom possibly the rise of humanitarian ideas not only tends to counteract the weeding out of the unfit, but even makes it relatively easy for them to propagate their species. What the result of the intermarriage of cousins is when war, famine, and infanticide are efficient weeders out of the unfit, we cannot say. Possibly or even probably the ill results would be inappreciable. It must not be forgotten that the marriage of near relatives is only harmful because or if it hands on to the children of the union an hereditary taint in a strengthened form, a result which is likely to follow in civilised life because hereditary taints are allowed to flourish unchecked by prudence and controlled by natural selection only so far as humanitarianism will permit it. These hereditary degeneracies however are probably largely if not entirely absent among savages. It is therefore open to question how far intermarriage of cousins would prove harmful under such conditions.

Statistics of the influence of cousin-marriage are not however what Mr Morgan wants. It is essential for him to prove that father-daughter marriage is more harmful than brother-sister unions.

It might be imagined that the data for estimating the effect of the union of father and daughter would be non-existent, but this is not so. Within the last few years it has been stated that such unions are common in parts of South America, and that the children, so far from being degenerates, are remarkably healthy and vigorous[1]. This is of interest in connection with Mr Atkinson's speculations as to the history of the family. In this connection it may be pointed out that such unions, *ex hypothesi*, are unlikely to result in continual in-and-in breeding, and would in all probability seldom be continued beyond the first alliance of this nature.

We are practically in complete darkness as to the results of brother and sister marriage in the human species. We have of course various cases of ruling families who perpetuated themselves in this way, but the data from such peoples refer to an advanced stage of culture and to a favoured class. They are not therefore applicable to similar unions among savages where they formed, as Mr Morgan suggests, the invariable practice. It is however possible to deduce from very simple considerations the probabilities as to the respective effects of adelphic and father-daughter unions. In the first place, as has been already pointed out, the father-daughter union implies only one family of in-and-in-bred children; in the case of brother and sister marriage, on the other hand, this state of things may go on indefinitely. If this is not enough to turn the scale against adelphic unions there is the further fact that, taking the descendants of the first pair of intermarrying descendants of common parents, whose tendency to disease or deformity is we will suppose $x^1$ on both sides, and assuming that this tendency increases in a simple ratio, the offspring have the same tendencies to the second power of x. If their children marry each other the measure of degeneracy in the third generation is $x^4$. Suppose now a father and mother with index of degeneracy each $x^1$; a daughter of this union will have as her index $x^2$; if the daughter bears children to the father, their index will be not $x^4$, but $x^3$, if the simple law which I have assumed for the purposes of argument holds good.

It is therefore clear that the offspring of adelphic unions, so far from being at an advantage compared with the offspring of

[1] *Wiener Med. Wochenschrift*, 1904; cf. *Fort. Rev.* LXXXIII, 460, n. 18. There is, as Mr Lang informs me, a curious Panama case in records of the Darien expedition, 1699.

father-daughter unions, are at a disadvantage in the proportion of 4 to 3. In the third place, in father-daughter unions the male is physically as well as sexually mature. In adelphic unions both parties are probably immature. Consequently from this point of view also the advantage is with the supposed injurious type of union. Now if the father-daughter union was less harmful than the brother-sister union, *a fortiori* are uncle-niece and similar unions less harmful. Yet Morgan supposes them to have been prohibited in favour of brother and sister unions.

Mr Morgan's reformation therefore turns out to have been no reformation at all, but a retrograde step. Assuming however that the facts were as he supposed them to be, and that the reformation was a real one, it is by no means clear how he supposes it to have been brought about. It was, as we have seen, an unconscious[1] reformation ; it is not supposed therefore that the primeval savage detected more pronounced signs of degeneracy in the offspring of one class of union and by the force of public opinion caused such unions to fall into disrepute and ultimately into desuetude. So far as can be seen the method which Mr Morgan had in his mind was this: certain unions resulted in offspring less able to maintain the struggle for existence, and these families consequently tended to die out. Other unions—those of sisters and brothers—on the other hand produced more vigorous children, and tended to perpetuate themselves. Whereas originally there was no tendency either one way or the other, some families developed from unknown causes, which, whatever they were, were neither moral nor utilitarian, the practice of brother and sister marriage. This diathesis followed the ordinary laws of descent, and eventually those families which were fortunate enough to be affected in that way exterminated their rivals.

Now, as will be shown immediately, this course of events seems to be in contradiction with the facts of savage society at the present day and with all probability. Apart from that however, how does Mr Morgan suppose his eugenic diathesis to be transmitted? It can hardly be maintained that this was

[1] Sometimes but usually not, for Morgan is utterly inconsistent.

the result of the different social conditions of the families in which brothers and sisters intermarried. Obviously there would be nothing to prevent the male in one of these unions from reverting to the other type of marriage. This would indeed be highly probable for reasons to be developed in the next paragraph. But if social conditions were not the determining factor, we are left with the somewhat grotesque theory of innate ideas. It is hardly necessary to refute this origin of social evolution.

Perhaps the strongest objection, however, to Mr Morgan's theory is the fact that in the most primitive communities the female tends to be younger, often much younger, than her mate. It is a readily ascertainable fact, though it seems to have been neglected by Mr Morgan, that the age of puberty does not coincide with the greatest development of the physical powers, but precedes it in the human subject by many years. The result of this is that the younger males are, as a rule, in the case of many mammals, held in subjection by the patriarch of the herd, the result being what I have termed above patriarchal polygyny, as long as the old male retains his powers. We have, it is true, no evidence of any such conditions among the anthropoids; but it must not be forgotten that we have no evidence of the consanguine family either among anthropoids, other mammals or human beings.

It tells against the hypothesis of patriarchal polygyny that both among horses and among camels there is evidence of the existence of actual sexual aversion between both sire and filly and dam and colt in the first case; and, as Aristotle tells us, at least between dam and colt in the case of camels; but we can hardly argue from Ungulata to Primates.

However this may be, the objections to Morgan's theories do not lose their strength. Enough has perhaps been said of them from the point of view of theory. We may look at them in the light of the known facts of social evolution among races of low stages of culture.

If we now turn for a moment to see what light Australian facts throw on the first two stages postulated by Mr Morgan, we find that the theoretical objections are amply supported by the course of evolution which can be traced in Australian social regulations. It will be recollected that in his view father-daughter marriage disappeared first, then brother and sister marriage. Totemism apart, there are in Australia, as we have seen, two kinds of organisation for the regulation of marriage—phratries, the dichotomous division of the southern tribes, and classes, the four-fold or eight-fold division of the other areas as to which we have any knowledge. Of these the phratry is demonstrably older than the class. But the result of the division of a tribe into two phratries is to prevent brother and sister marriage, while, so far as phratry rules are concerned, father and daughter are still free to marry in those tribes where the descent is matrilineal. The result (though not necessarily the original object) of the class-system, on the other hand, is to prevent the marriage of fathers and daughters and generally of the older generation with the younger, so far as the classes actually represent generations. In actual practice the class into which a man may marry includes females of all ages, so that he is only debarred from marrying young females if they are his own daughters. But if we may assume that the original object of the classes was to prevent the intermarriage of different generations, it is at once obvious that in Australia the evolution postulated by Mr Morgan, if it took place at all, took place in reverse order, the brother and sister marriage being the first to be brought under the ban.

The objections to which attention has been called seem to make it difficult if not impossible to accept Morgan's explanations either of the processes or of the causes which led to the passage from promiscuity to communal marriage.

# CHAPTER XII.

## GROUP MARRIAGE AND THE TERMS OF RELATIONSHIP.

Mother and Child. Kurnai terms. Dieri evidence. *Noa.* Group Mothers. Classification and descriptive terms. Poverty of language. Terms express status. The savage view natural.

WE may now turn to consider the terms of relationship from the point of view of marriage, more especially in connection with Australia. We have already seen that there are great difficulties in the way of Morgan's hypothesis that the names accurately represent the relations which formerly existed in the tribes which used them. I propose to discuss the matter here from a somewhat different standpoint.

It seems highly probable that if any individual term came into use, whether monogamy, patriarchal polygyny, "group marriage," or promiscuity prevailed, it would be that which expresses the relationship of a mother to her child. The only other possibility would be that in the first two conditions mentioned the relation of husband to wife might take precedence.

In actual practice we find that the name which a mother applies to her own child is applied by her equally to the children of the women whom her husband might have married. This state of things may obviously arise from one of three causes. (*a*) In the first place the name may have been originally that which a mother applied to her own son, and it may have been extended to those who were her nephews in a state of monogamy, or stepsons (= sons of other women by the same father) in a state of polygyny either with or without polyandry. (*b*) The theory that a name was applied originally to own and collateral relatives has already been discussed, so far as it refers to the "undivided commune." The case of regulated promiscuity is different and must be considered here. (*c*) On the other hand the name which she uses may have been expressive of tribal status or group status, and may have had nothing to do with descent.

It is unnecessary to say much about the first of these possibilities. First, there is no evidence to show that such a thing has taken place; secondly, we can see no reason why such a thing should take place; thirdly, if such a change of meaning did take place, it is quite clear that we have no grounds for regarding the philological evidence for group marriage as having the slightest significance.

In connection with the second hypothesis—that the names actually represent the relations formerly existing, it may be well to preface the discussion by a few remarks on the regulation of marriage in Australia. The rules by which the Australian native is bound, when he sets out to choose a wife, make the area of choice as a rule dependent on his status, that is to say, he must, in order to find a wife, go to another phratry, class, totem-kin, or combination of two of these, membership of which depends on descent, direct or indirect; on the other hand he may be limited by regulations dependent on locality, that is to say he may have to take a wife from a group resident in a certain area. There is reason to suppose that the latter regulations are the outcome of earlier status regulations which have fallen into desuetude. However this may be, all that we are here concerned with is the fact that regulations in this case also are virtually dependent on descent, inasmuch as a man is not in practice free to reside where he likes, but remains in his own group, though occasionally he joins that of his wife (this does not apparently affect the exogamic rule). The groups are therefore to all intents and purposes totem-kins with male descent.

Taking the Kurnai as our example of the non-class-organised groups, we find that the fraternal relationship once started goes on for ever; the result of this is that with few exceptions the whole of the intermarrying groups, so far as they are of the same generation, are brothers and sisters. Dr Howitt, whose authority on matters of Australian ethnology is final, recognises that on the principles on which group marriage is deduced from terms of relationship, this fact should point to the Kurnai being yet in the stage of the undivided commune (why, it is difficult to see, when they are definitely exogamous), but regards the argument from terms of relationship as untrustworthy in this instance. If it is not reliable in one case it may well be unreliable in all; we are entitled to ask supporters of the hypothesis of group marriage what differentiates this case from those in which they have no doubt of the validity of the philological argument.

Now if Dr Howitt's doubts as to the interpretation to be put upon the Kurnai terms of relationship are correct, we may reasonably, in the absence of proof that they originated in a different way from the Malayan terms, ask ourselves upon what basis the case for promiscuity rests. Beyond a few customs, and it will be shown below that it is unnecessary to regard them as survivals of a period when marriage was unknown, the proof is purely philological, and on examination the philological proof is found to be wanting.

Dr Howitt, in his recent book, rests the case for the undivided commune (i.e. promiscuity) on the Australian terms of relationship which he discusses, viz. those of the Dieri and the Kurnai. He will not admit that the Kurnai terms point to the undivided commune; we are therefore left with the Dieri terms. But the Dieri organisation, so far from being that of an undivided commune, is the two-phratry arrangement by which a man is by no means free to marry any woman in his tribe, but is limited to one-half of the women; further, tribal customs limit his choice still further and compel him to marry his mother's mother's brother's daughter's daughter (these terms do not refer to blood but so-called "tribal" relationship, i.e. it is a woman with a certain tribal status whom he has to marry). Where then does Dr Howitt find his proof of promiscuity?

We have, it is true, a certain number of tribal legends, according to which the phratry organisation was instituted to prevent the marriage of too near kin. But, quite apart from the fact that tribal legends are not evidence, the legends merely point to a period when marriage was unregulated, when a man was free to marry any woman, not when he was *de facto* or *de jure* the husband of every woman. Even if it be proved beyond question that marriage was once unregulated, it does not follow that promiscuity prevailed.

The existence of the undivided commune is a proof of promiscuity only for those who discover proofs of group marriage in the divided commune, in other words in the terms of relationship and the customs of the ordinary two-phratry tribe of the present day. We may therefore let the decision of the question of the validity of terms of relationship as a proof of extensive connubial activities rest upon the discussion of the evidence to be drawn from the tribes selected by Dr Howitt and Messrs Spencer and Gillen, viz. the Dieri and the Urabunna.

It may however be pointed out that neither of these writers has dealt with the passage from promiscuity to "group marriage," nor shown how under the former system terms of relationship could come into existence at all. With the difficulties we have dealt above.

We must now revert to the question of the origin of the so-called "terms of relationship." Are they expressive of kinship or only of status and duties? Neither Lewis Morgan nor the authorities on Australian marriage customs—Dr Howitt and Messrs Spencer and Gillen—discuss the question at length, but seem to regard it as an axiom (although they warn us that all European ideas of relationship must be dismissed when we deal with the classificatory system) that all these terms may be interpreted on the hypothesis that the European relationships to which they most nearly correspond actually existed in former times, not, as in Europe, between individuals, but between groups. The case on which Spencer and Gillen rely is that of the *unawa* relationship. They argue that a man is *unawa* to a whole group of women, one of whom is his individual wife; for this individual wife no special name exists, she is just *unawa* (= *noa*) like all the other women he might have married. Consequently the marital relation must have existed formerly between the man in question and the whole group of *unawa* women. The reasoning does not seem absolutely conclusive, and our doubts as to the validity of the argument are strengthened when we apply it to another case and find the results inconsistent with facts which are known to the lowest savage. Not only has a man only one name for the women he might have married, and for the woman he actually did marry, but a mother has only one name for the son she actually bore, and for the sons of the women who, if they had become her husband's wives, would have borne him sons in her stead. From this fact by parity of reasoning we must draw the obvious conclusion that during the period when group marriage was the rule, individual mothers were unknown. If we are entitled to conclude from the fact that a man's wife bears the same name for him as all the other women whom he might have married, that he at one time was the husband of them all, then we are obviously equally entitled to conclude, from the fact that a woman's son is known to her by the same name as the sons of other women, either that during the period of group marriage she actually bore the sons of the other women or that the whole group of women produced their sons by their joint efforts. Finding that the term which is translated "son" is equally applied by the remainder of the group of women to the son of the individual woman, whose case we have been considering, we may discard the former hypothesis and come to the conclusion that if there was a period of group marriage there was also one of group motherhood. This interesting fact may be commended to the attention of zoologists.

It is perhaps unnecessary to pursue the argument any further. The single point on which Spencer and Gillen rely is sufficiently refuted by a single *reductio ad absurdum*. If more proof is needed it may be found in Dr Howitt's work[1]. We learn from him that a man is the younger brother of his maternal grandmother, and consequently the maternal grandfather of his second cousin. Surely it is not possible in this case to contend that the "terms of relationship" are expressive of anything but duties and status. It seems unreasonable to maintain in the

[1] p. 163.

interests of an hypothesis that a man can be his own great uncle and the son of more than one mother.

From the foregoing discussion it will be clear that there are very grave, if not insurmountable, difficulties in the way of regarding the "terms of relationship" as being in reality such. In reply to those who regard them as status terms it is urged that if they are not terms of relationship, then the savages have no terms of any sort to express relationships which we regard as obvious, the implication being that this is unthinkable.

Now in the first place it may be pointed out that the converse is certainly true. Civilised man has a large number of terms of relationship, but he has none for such ideas as *noa*; a boy has no term for all men who might have been his father; a woman has no name for the children of all women who might have married her husband, if she had not anticipated them. To the savage this is just as unthinkable as the converse seems to be to some civilised men.

In the second place it is perfectly obvious that the savage has, as a matter of fact, no names for the quite unmistakeable relationship of mother and child. The name which an Australian mother applies to her son, she applies equally to the sons of all other women of her own status; the name which a son applies to his mother, he applies equally to all the women of her status, whether married or unmarried, in old age, middle life, youth, or infancy. If there is no term for this relation we can hardly argue that the absence of terms for other relations is unthinkable.

Morgan attempted to meet this objection by urging that in a state of promiscuity a woman would apply the same name to the children of other women as to her own, because they were or might be by the same father. But in the first place this assumes that the relationship to the father was considered rather than the relationship to the mother, and this is against all analogy. In the second place, even granting Morgan's postulate, the relation of a mother to her son is not that of a wife to the children of other wives of a polygynous husband. Poverty of language is therefore established in this case, and may be taken for granted where the obvious relationships are concerned.

It has been pointed out more than once that there are grave difficulties in the way of any hypothesis which assumes that terms of relationship, properly so called, were evolved in a state of pure promiscuity. It has now been shown that no intelligible account of the meaning of such terms can be given, even if we dismiss the difficulties just mentioned and assume that terms were somehow or other evolved, and a transition effected to a state of regulated promiscuity. If on the other hand we regard the "terms of relationship" as originally indicative of tribal status and suppose they have been transformed in the course of ages into "descriptive" terms such as we use in everyday life, the difficulties vanish.

For one proof of this hypothesis we need look no further than the terms of relationship applied by a mother to her own (and other) children, an illustration which has already done duty more than once. It is abundantly clear that what this term expresses is not relationship but status, the relation of one generation to the next in the Malayan system, of the half of a generation to the next generation in the same moiety of the tribe among the Dieri, and so on.

It is admitted even by believers in group marriage that the terms of relationship do not correspond to anything actually existing; beyond the "survivals" which we shall consider below, they can produce no shadow of proof that the terms ever did correspond to actual relationships, as they understand them. They can give no proof whatever that they did not express status.

It is therefore a fair hypothesis that *unawa* (*noa*) and similar terms express status and not relationship. From the example of mother and son we see that the Australian does not select for distinction by a special term that bond which is most obvious both to him and us. It is therefore by no means surprising that by *unawa* he should mean, not the existence of marital relations, but their possibility, from a 'legal' point of view. Just as he is struck, not by the genetic relation between mother and son, but by the fact that they belong to different generations, so in the case of husband and wife the *existence* of marital relations between them is neglected, and the point selected for emphasis is the *legality* of such marital relations, whether existent or not.

It is singular that anyone should regard this savage view of life as anything but natural. For the Australian the due observance of the marriage regulations is a tribal matter; their breach, whether the connection be by marriage or free love, is a matter of more than private concern. The relations of a man with his legal wife however concern other members of the tribe but little. Public opinion among the Dieri, it is true, condemns the unfaithful wife, but her punishment is left to the husband; among the Kamilaroi the tribe indeed takes the matter up but only on the complaint of the husband; and generally speaking it is the husband who, possibly with his totemic brethren, pursues the abductor. We have therefore in this insistence on the legal status of the couple and the comparative indifference to the husband's rights a sufficiently exact parallel to the insistence on status and not marital relations in the use of the term *unawa*.

The course of evolution has been, not, as group-marriagers contend, from group to individual terms of relationship but from terms descriptive of status to terms descriptive of relationship.

It is, in fact, on any hypothesis, impossible to deny this. Whatever terms of relationship may have meant in the past, no believer in group marriage contends that they represent anything actually existing. But this is equivalent to admitting that they express status and not relationship, and no proof has ever been given that they were ever anything else.

# CHAPTER XIII.

## PIRRAURU.

Theories of group marriage. Meaning of group. Dieri customs. Tippa-malku marriage. Obscure points. *Pirrauru*. Obscure points. Relation of *pirrauru* to *tippa-malku* unions. Kurnandaburi. Wakelbura customs. Kurnai organisation. Position of widow. *Piraungaru* of Urabunna. *Pirrauru* and group marriage. *Pirrauru* not a survival. Result of scarcity of women. Duties of *Pirrauru* spouses. *Piraungaru*; obscure points.

WE now come to the marriage customs of the Australian natives of the present day and the supposed survivals of group marriage. In dealing with the question of group marriage we are met with a preliminary difficulty. No one has formulated a definition of this state, and the interpretations of the term are very diverse.

Fison, for example, says[1] group marriage does not necessarily imply actual giving in marriage or cohabitation; all it means is a marital right or rather qualification which comes by birth. He argues however on a later page[2] that Nair polyandry, which is more properly termed promiscuity, is group marriage. Much the same view is taken by A. H. Post[3], who regards the theory of pure promiscuity and the undivided commune as untenable.

Kohler, on the other hand[4], speaks of group marriage as existing among the Omahas, a patrilineal tribe, be it remarked; but means by that no more than adelphic polygyny.

[1] *Aust. Ass.* IV, 689.
[2] *Ib.* p. 717.
[3] *Ausland*, 1891, p. 843.
[4] *Zts. Vgl. Rechtsw.* XII, 268.

Spencer and Gillen criticise Westermarck's use of the term "pretended group marriage" and assert it to be a fact among the Urabunna. On the very next page group marriage is spoken of as having preceded the present state of things. Both statements cannot be true.

For the purposes of the present work I understand group marriage to mean promiscuity limited by regulations based on organisations such as age-grades, phratries, totem-kins, or local groups.

The fact is that Spencer and Gillen and other writers on Australia use the term group merely as a noun of multitude. They do not mean by group, in one sense, anything more than a number of persons. In this sense they speak of group marriage (= polygamy) at the present day—a fact which is not peculiar to Australia and which no one is concerned to deny. By a quite illegitimate transformation of meaning they also apply the term group to a portion of a tribe distinguished by a class name and (or or) term of relationship and mean by group marriage class promiscuity. They do not even perceive that they make this transition, for otherwise Messrs Spencer and Gillen could hardly assail Dr Westermarck for using the term "pretended group marriage" which is quite accurate as a description of group (= class) marriage or promiscuity. Even if there were justification for assuming that group marriage (= polygamy) is a lineal descendant of group marriage (= class promiscuity), nothing would be gained by using the term group marriage of both. In the subsequent discussion it will be made clear that whatever their causal connection, there is hardly a single point of similarity between them beyond the fact that the sexual relations are in neither case monogamous. It is therefore to be hoped that the supporters of the hypothesis of group marriage will in the future encourage clear thinking by not using the same term for different forms of sexual union.

I now proceed to discuss the alleged survival of group marriage and other Australian marriage customs.

Taking the Dieri tribe as our example the following state of things is found to prevail. The tribe is divided into exogamous moieties, Matteri and Kararu; subject to restrictions dependent on kinship, with which we are not immediately concerned, any Matteri may marry any Kararu. A reciprocal term, *noa*[1], is in use to denote the status of those who may marry each other. This *noa* relationship is sometimes cited as a proof of the existence of group marriage. As a matter of fact it is no more evidence of group marriage than the fact that a man is *noa* to all the unmarried women of England except a few, is proof of the existence of group marriage in England; or the fact that *femme* in French means both wife and woman is an argument for the existence of promiscuity in France in Roman or post-Roman times.

A ceremony, usually performed in infancy or childhood, changes the relationship of a *noa* male and female from *noa-mara* to *tippa-malku*. The step is taken by the mothers with the concurrence of the girl's maternal uncles, and is in fact betrothal. Apparently no further ceremony is necessary to constitute a marriage. At any rate nothing is said as to that.

In connection with this form of marriage there are two points of importance to be noted. The first is that whereas a man may have as many *tippa-malku* wives as he can get, a woman cannot have more than one *tippa-malku* husband, at any rate not at the same time. After the husband's death she may again enter into the *tippa-malku* relation. The second point is that the *tippa-malku* relation must precede the *pirrauru* relation, of which I shall speak in a moment, and cannot succeed it[2].

There are unfortunately many points in Dr Howitt's narrative which demand elucidation. He says, for example, that *noa* individuals become "*tippa-malku* for the time being[3]." This suggests, probably erroneously, that the *tippa-malku* relation is merely temporary; but I am unable to say whether it in reality means that the *tippa-malku* relation is terminated by the capture of the woman, or that divorce is practised and may terminate the relationship at the will of the man only or of both parties.

[1] The statement, *Journ. Anthr. Inst.* XX, 55, that a man and woman become *noa* by betrothal is clearly erroneous.

[2] *Nat. Tribes*, p. 181. This was not brought out by Dr Howitt's paper of 1890 in *Journ. Anthr. Inst.* XX, and is denied in *Folklore* XVII, 174 sq. by Dr Howitt himself; see my criticism, *ib.* 294 sq.

[3] p. 179.

Another point on which we have no information is the position of the unmarried girls and widows. Free love is permitted, the only limitation[1] given by Dr Howitt being that the man (who must of course have passed through the Mindari ceremony) must not be *tippa-malku* to the girl, but must be *noa-mara*. It would be interesting to know whether girls in the *tippa-malku* relation before actual marriage are at liberty to have sexual relations with any men of the right status or only with unmarried men, or whether the privilege is restricted to those who are not yet *tippa-malku* to any one, and how far the same restriction applies to the men.

Any man who has been duly initiated, whether he is married to a *tippa-malku* wife or not, and any woman who has a *tippa-malku* husband[2], can enter or be put into a relation termed *pirrauru* with one or more persons of the opposite sex. The effect of the ceremony—termed *kandri*—is to give to the *pirrauru* spouses the position of subsidiary husbands and wives, whose rights take precedence of the *tippa-malku* rights at tribal gatherings, but at other times can only be exercised in the absence of the *tippa-malku* spouse, or, when the male is unmarried, with the permission of the *tippa-malku* husband of the *pirrauru* spouse.

The *pirrauru* relation is, for the woman, a modification of a previously existing *tippa-malku* marriage; that being so, it cannot be quoted as evidence of a more pristine state of things in which she was by birth the legal and actual spouse of all men of a certain tribal status.

The *pirrauru* relation falls under two heads of the classification I have given above, according as the man has or has not a *tippa-malku* wife. In the first case, it is, taken in combination with the *tippa-malku* marriage, a case of bi-lateral adelphic dissimilar (M. and F.) polygamy. In the latter it is dissimilar adelphic (tribal) polyandry, adelphic being taken here, be it noted, in the sense of tribal, and possibly, but not necessarily, own brother.

[1] p. 187. Subject to the girl having passed the *wilpadrina* ceremony. *Journ. Anthr. Inst.* XX, 56.

[2] But see p. 129, n. 2.

Here too our information is unfortunately fragmentary and sometimes contradictory. We learn from Dr Howitt, for example, that a *pirrauru* is always a brother's wife or a wife's sister (they are usually the same), and the relation arises through the exchange by brothers of their wives[1]. But on the next page we learn that the unmarried (men) can also become *pirraurus*. It appears further that a woman may ask for a *pirrauru*, but whether he must be a married man or not is not clear. It is only stated that she has to get her husband to consent to the arrangement. Further we find that important men have many *pirrauru* wives, but it does not appear how far they reciprocate the attention. Then again we are told that when two new *pirrauru* pairs are allotted to each other, all the other pairs are re-allotted. Are we to understand from this that the allocation of new *pirraurus* is a rare event or that the *pirrauru* relationship is a very temporary affair? Or does re-allotted simply mean that the names are called over? If the latter, the terminology is very unfortunate. Gason's statement is perfectly clear: once a *pirrauru*, always a *pirrauru*[2]. Again does it imply that the wishes[3] of the already existing *pirraurus* are consulted in the matter or not? If, as is stated, there is a good deal of jealousy between *pirraurus*, especially when one of them (the male) is unmarried, it is difficult to make the two statements fit in with one another. Once more, it is said that a widower takes his brother's wife as his *pirrauru*, giving presents to his brother. Does this imply that the consent of the husband is not necessary, or that he cannot refuse it, or that it is purchased? Again we read "a man is privileged to obtain a number of wives from his *noas* in common with the other men of his group, while a woman's wish can only be carried out with the consent of her *tippa-malku* husband." This latter statement clearly implies that a man can obtain a *pirrauru* without

[1] This is in contradiction with the statement (*Journ. Anthr. Inst.* XX, 56) that the various couples are not consulted. We also learn (*loc. cit.* p. 62) that the exercise of marital rights by own tribal brothers is independent of their *pirrauru* relation. The order of precedence is (1) *tippa-malku*, (2) *pirrauru*, (3) brothers.

[2] *Journ. Anthr. Inst.* XX, 57.

[3] Howitt says (p. 182) that each of a pair of *pirrauru* watch each other carefully to prevent more *pirrauru* relations arising.

the consent of the *tippa-malku* husband, but this contradicts what has already been told us about the exchange by brothers of their wives. Exchange is clearly not the right term to apply; if one or perhaps both have no voice in the matter, it is rather a transfer. These are by no means all the unsettled questions on which light is needed. What, for example, is the position of a *pirrauru* wife whose *tippa-malku* husband dies? Does she pass to a new *tippa-malku* husband? If so, must he be an ex-*pirrauru*? Does she continue in the *pirrauru* relation to her former *pirraurus*, regardless of her new husband's wishes? Can the *pirrauru* relationship be dissolved at the wish of either or both parties and by what means?

With so many obscurities in the narrative we must esteem ourselves fortunate that we are not left without the information that a special ceremony is necessary to make the *pirrauru* relation legal; this is performed by the head or heads of the men's totems, and need not be described here.

With regard to precedence it should be noted that at ordinary times the *tippa-malku* spouse always takes precedence of the *pirrauru* spouse. Where two men are *pirrauru* to the same woman, the *tippa-malku* husband being absent, the elder man may take the precedence or may share his rights and duties with the younger. It is the duty of the *pirrauru* husband to protect a woman during the absence of her *tippa-malku* husband.

A woman cannot refuse to take a *pirrauru* who has been regularly allotted to her. In her *tippa-malku* husband's absence the *pirrauru* husband takes his place as a matter of right. He cannot however take her away from the *tippa-malku* husband without his consent except at certain ceremonial times[1]. One other fact may be noted. An influential man hires out his *pirraurus* to those who have none.

Before we proceed to discuss the import of these facts it will be well to mention the analogous customs of the only two tribes outside the Dieri nation where the same relation is asserted to exist, and certain cases regarded by Dr Howitt, wrongly in all

[1] In the Urabunna tribe a woman is lent irrespective of *piraungaru* to all *nupa*, *Nor. Tr.* p. 63. It is therefore a matter of no moment even if the consent of the primary husband is never refused at non-ceremonial times.

probability, as on the same level as the *pirrauru* custom. In the Kurnandaburi, according to an informant of Dr Howitt's, a group of men who are own or tribal brothers and a group of women who are own or tribal sisters, are united, apparently without any ceremony, in group marriage, whenever the tribe assembles or this Dippa-malli group meets at other times[1].

Dr Howitt adds that in this tribe the husband often has an intrigue with his sister-in-law (wife's sister or brother's wife), although they are in the relation of *Kodi-molli* and practise a modified avoidance. This he attempts to equate with Dieri group marriage. It is not however clear that it is more than what we have called a liaison. Our authority does not state that it is recognised as lawful by public opinion, nor yet that any ceremony initiates the relations[2]. In the absence of these details we cannot regard his view as probable. It may however be noted that the widow in this tribe passes to the brother.

The only other case of "group marriage" which Dr Howitt gives[3] is in the Wakelbura tribe of C. Queensland. Here however, so far from being group marriage, it is, according to his own statement, simply adelphic polyandry. A man's unmarried brothers have marital rights and duties, the child is said to term them its father. It may however be pointed out that this hardly bears on the question of group marriage, for it would do so even if no marital relations existed between its mother and any other man besides the primary husband.

It will be seen that our information is very fragmentary, and what we have is neither precise nor free from contradiction.

[1] It appears, however (*Journ. Anthr. Inst.* XX, 62), to be only on ceremonial (Muni) occasions that anything like general intercourse occurs, termed Wira-jinka, then it is promiscuous. The Dippa-malli relation is not permanent (*Journ. Anthr. Inst.* XX, 61), and the *mebaia* husband receives a present. If the Dippa-malli "group" is not permanent, it does not appear why Dr Howitt speaks of a "group" at all.

[2] In the absence of these there is nothing to distinguish the practice from the adultery which prevails among the Dieri (p. 187), in which Dr Howitt does *not* see a survival of group marriage or promiscuity.

[3] He mentions the *pira* marriage of the Yandairunga in *Journ. Anthr. Inst.* XX, 60, but drops it in *Native Tribes*. It is unfortunate that we never learn why Dr Howitt omits to mention facts which he has previously published. Are we to infer that the previous statements are erroneous in every case? If so, *pirrauru* must be a temporary relationship.

A most essential point, for example, is the connection of the totem-kin with the *pirrauru* relationship. Among the Dieri the men may be of different totems. Is this the case among the Wakelbura? Was it always the case among the Dieri?

Before we leave Dr Howitt's work it is necessary to refer again to the Kurnai. The most important point in connection with the Kurnai, so far as the present work is concerned, is that, contradictory to Bulmer's statement[1] that unmarried men have access to their brothers' wives, and sometimes even married men, Dr Howitt mentions[2] as a singular fact that he recalls one instance of a wife being lent in that tribe.

Dr Howitt however holds that there are traces of group marriage in the tribe, and refers to the fact that the term *maian*[3] is applied to a wife by her husband and by his brother, whose "official wife[4]" she is thus declared to be, and that a brother takes his deceased brother's widow. He regards this rather unfortunately named custom of the levirate as having its root in group marriage. Now *maian* is applied, not only by a husband to a wife, but by a wife to her husband's sister, and by a sister to her brother's wife. If therefore the use of the term proves anything, it proves, not group marriage, as Dr Howitt understands it, but promiscuity, the prior existence of the undivided commune, and this, as we have seen, Dr Howitt declines to accept on the strength of the philological argument.

We are therefore reduced to the levirate as a proof of the former existence of group marriage. But there is nothing whatever to show that it is not a case of inheritance of property. For the Australians, as for many other savage peoples, the married state is the only thinkable one for the adult, and that being so it is natural for the widow to remarry. She has however been purchased by the exchange of a woman in the relation of sister to the deceased, and if the widow were allowed to pass to another group, the property thus acquired would be alienated. Moreover the marriage regulations require the woman

[1] Curr, III. [2] *Journ. Anthr. Inst.* XX, 61, n. 2.

[3] Dr Howitt's argument from the use of *maian* raises a difficulty. Twenty-five years ago he stated (Brough Smyth, II, 323) that among the Brabrolung a wife was termed *wrŭkŭt*, and this seems to be the ordinary term.

[4] Titular *maian* is Dr Howitt's phrase.

to marry only a tribal brother of the deceased. It is therefore in every way natural for a brother to succeed to a brother. No arguments for the prior existence of group marriage can be founded on the levirate, any more than an argument for primitive communism can be founded on other laws of inheritance. At most the *maian* relationship is evidence of adelphic polygyny[1].

For the Urabunna we depend on the information gained by Spencer and Gillen on their first expedition. Here the circle from which a man takes his wife is much more restricted than among the Dieri. Not only is he bound to choose a woman of the other moiety of the tribe, but he is restricted to a certain totem[2] in that moiety, and to the daughters of his mother's elder brothers (tribal) in that totem. Hence although the *kami* relationship of the Dieri is unknown among the Urabunna, the choice among the latter is more limited.

The marriageable group is termed *nupa* by both men and women; in addition to the *nupa* relationship and the unnamed individual marriage, into which a man enters with one or more of his *nupa*, there is the *piraungaru* relationship, corresponding to the *pirrauru* of the Dieri. In each case the elder brothers of the woman decide who are to have the primary and who the secondary right to the female. In the case of the *piraungaru* however the matter requires confirmation by the old men of the tribe. The circumstances under which the *piraungaru* claims take the first rank are not stated by Messrs Spencer and Gillen; the statement that a man lends his *piraungaru* need not, of course, refer to times at which he himself cannot claim the right of access[3].

We may now turn to a discussion of the bearing of the facts just cited on the question of "group marriage." The first point is naturally that of nomenclature, and we at once recognise that among the Dieri the relations of the *pirrauru* are not marriage,

[1] Dr Howitt's statement on p. 281 that the widow invariably passes to the brother is contradicted by passages on pp. 227 and 248.

[2] Dr Howitt (p. 176) does not admit this to be correct, but cf. his attitude on p. 188.

[3] But cf. *Journ. Anthr. Inst.* XX, 58 n.; this may, however, have been regarded as a ceremonial occasion, though there is no other evidence of such being the case.

either on the definition suggested by Dr Westermarck or on that given in Chapter XI of the present work. If two *tippa-malku* pairs are reciprocally in *pirrauru*, the only relations between them, unless the *tippa-malku* husbands absent themselves or are complaisant, are, strictly speaking, those of temporary regulated polygamy or promiscuity, and rather a restriction than an extension of similar customs in other tribes, as I shall show below.

A second point of a similar nature is that the parties to a *pirrauru* union are in no sense a group[1]. They are not united by any bond, local, totemistic, tribal, or otherwise. The theoretical "group marriage"—the union of all the *noa*—does, in a sense, refer to a group, though this term properly refers rather to a body of people distinguished by residence or some other *local* differentia from other persons or groups. But no distinction of this kind can in any sense be affirmed of the *pirrauru* spouses; it cannot be said of them that they are in any way distinguished from the remainder of their tribe, phratry, class or totem-kin. From this it follows that the term class-marriage cannot be applied to the relation between the *pirrauru*, nor yet class promiscuity; the *pirrauru*, though members of a certain class, do not include all members of that class.

Turning now to the custom itself, let us examine how far it presents any marks of being a survival of a previous state of class promiscuity. *Pirrauru* relations are regarded by Dr Howitt and others as survivals from a previous stage of "group," by which we must, presumably, understand class or status marriage, or promiscuity. So far as they are evidence of this, the *pirrauru* customs are certainly important. If however it cannot be shown that they probably point to some form of promiscuity, they have but little importance except as a freak or exceptional development of polyandry and polygyny.

Let us recall the distinguishing features of the *pirrauru* union. They are (1) consent of the husband (?); (2) recognition

[1] Properly speaking group marriage should mean that all persons in a local group live in polygamy, a state not far removed indeed from promiscuity, the boundary between which and polygamy I cannot undertake to discuss here, or else that the whole of one group is united in marriage to those of the opposite sex in another group.

by the totem-kin through its head-man; (3) temporary character[1]; (4) priority of the *tippa-malku* union in the case of the woman; (5) purchase of *pirrauru* rights by (*a*) the brother who becomes a widower, and (*b*) visitors or others without *pirraurus* of their own, the rights being in the latter case for a very short period and not dependent on recognition by the totem-kin, so far as Dr Howitt's narrative is a guide. Now unless "group marriage" was very different from what it is commonly represented to be, the essence of it was that all the men of one class had sexual rights over the women of another class. How far does this picture coincide with the features of the *pirrauru*, which is regarded as a survival of it? In the first place *pirrauru* is created by a ceremony, which is performed, not by the head, nor even in the Wakelbura tribe, by a member of the supposed intermarried classes of the earlier period; but by the heads of the totem-kins of the individual men concerned. Now it is quite unthinkable that the right of class promiscuity, to use the correct term, should ever have been exercised subject to any such restriction; even were it otherwise the performance of the ceremony would more naturally fall into the hands of tribal, phratriac, or class authorities than of the heads of totem-kins. Then too if *pirrauru* is a survival of group marriage we should expect the ceremony to be performed for the *tippa-malku* union and not for the *pirrauru*.

Again if *tippa-malku* is later and *pirrauru* earlier, what is the meaning of the regulation that the woman must first be united in *tippa-malku* marriage before she can enter into the *pirrauru* relationship? On the "group marriage" theory this fact demands to be explained, no less than the different position of men and women in this respect. We have seen that freedom in sexual matters is accorded to both bachelors and spinsters. It is therefore from no sense of the value of chastity, from no jealousy of the future *tippa-malku* husband's rights, that the female is excluded from the *pirrauru* relation until she has a husband.

Again, if *pirrauru* is a relic of former rights, now restricted to a few of the group which formerly exercised them, why is the

[1] This is uncertain, as I have already intimated.

husband's consent needed before the *pirrauru* relation is set up, and why is the *pirrauru* relation, once established, not permanent (assuming that my reading of Dr Howitt is right)?

Once more, if *pirrauru* is a right, how comes it that a brother has to purchase the right, when he becomes a widower[1]? What too is the meaning of the transference of *pirrauru* women to strangers in return for gifts?

All these points seem to me to weigh heavily against the survival theory, and we may add to them the fact that the *tippa-malku* husband, so far from having to gain the consent of his fellows before he obtains his wife, gets her by arrangement with her mother and her mother's brothers, all of whom belong to the other moiety, and consequently are not among those whose supposed group rights are infringed by the introduction of individual marriage. When we consider that the *jus primae noctis* is explained as an expiation for individual marriage the position of the *tippa-malku* husband and the method in which he obtains his wife are exceedingly instructive.

Supporters of the theory of group marriage will naturally ask in what other way the facts can be explained. The unfortunate lack of detail to which I have alluded does not make it easier to make any counter-suggestion; but the explanation may, I think, be inferred from the facts already at our disposal. We have seen that in the Wakelbura tribe, so far from the condition being one of "group marriage," it is one of dissimilar adelphic polyandry. Now it is by no means easy to see how this could arise from the Dieri custom, the essence of which, according to one of the statements I have quoted, is reciprocity. On the other hand we can readily see how polyandry of this type, which is found in other parts of the world also, may be in Australia, as in other regions, the result of a scarcity of women[2], or, what is the same thing, of polygyny on the part of the notables of the tribe and of the independent custom of postponing the age of marriage in the male till 28 or 30.

[1] This tells strongly in favour of my theory. The unmarried youth gets his *pirrauru* free, for he will reciprocate the attention later. The man who has lost his wife and can make no return purchases the right.

[2] Cf. Curr, III, 546.

With this view agree the facts that in some cases the brother is required to purchase his *pirrauru* rights, that the young man without *pirrauru* wife can purchase from another man the temporary use of one of his *pirrauru* spouses, and that the *tippa-malku* marriage always precedes the *pirrauru* relation in the female. It may indeed be urged against the view that the purchase of a temporary *pirrauru* is in fact not a case of *pirrauru* at all, but simply the ordinary purchase of hospitality among savage nations. This is no doubt the case and we might merely cite this fact in order to show that the purchase of sexual rights is a recognised proceeding in Australia. Looked at from another point of view however the case is seen to be singularly instructive. So far as Dr Howitt's statements go, the husband of the *pirrauru* who is thus lent does not require to be consulted in the matter. The *pirrauru* husband, on the other hand, disposes of his spouse exactly as if she were a slave. On the theory of group marriage the *tippa-malku* husband has no less a right to be consulted in the matter than the *pirrauru* husband. In point of fact he seems to be entirely neglected in the transaction. It is true that in the case we are considering the *pirrauru* husband seems to have exceptional privileges, for we have seen that under ordinary circumstances the *tippa-malku* husband has exclusive rights at ordinary times. But we must probably understand the passage to mean that the lending of *pirraurus* takes place at tribal meetings[1] or on other occasions when the right of the husband is in abeyance. In either case, the facts tell far more strongly in favour of the view suggested here than in favour of group marriage.

There is another factor to be considered. Abductions and elopements are merely ordinary amenities of married life among the aborigines of Australia. We have seen that it is the duty of the *pirrauru* husband to protect the wife during the absence of the *tippa-malku* husband. Clearly this is a sort of insurance against the too bold suitor or the too fickle wife, unless indeed the *pirrauru* himself is the offender, a point on which Dr Howitt has nothing to say, though Mr Siebert's

[1] Cf. *Journ. Anthr. Inst.* XX, 73.

evidence may be fairly interpreted to mean that such occurrences are not known.

We shall see below in connection with the question of the *jus primae noctis* that special privileges are sometimes accorded to men of the husband's totem or class in return for assistance in capturing the wife. Now assuming that a wife is abducted or elopes, it is, I think, on the same persons that the duty of aiding the injured husband would fall. Whether this is so or not, the men of his own totem are those with whom a man's relations are, in most tribes, the closest. We have seen that the heads of the totem-kins play an important part in assigning *pirraurus*. Now although it is actually the practice for men of different totems to exchange wives, it by no means follows that it was always the case. The element of adelphic polyandry, for example, may well have upset the original relations and brought about a practice of exchange between men of different totems. At any rate the theory here suggested affords an explanation of the part played by the totem headmen, and on the theory of group marriage their share in the transaction remains absolutely mysterious.

In connection with these possible explanations of the *pirrauru* custom, it is important to observe that there are duties in regard to food owed by the *pirrauru* wife to her spouse, when her husband is absent. Now it is hardly conceivable that in a state of "group marriage" any such practice should have obtained. A woman would doubtless have collected food for the man with whom she was actually cohabiting; but in the case of the *pirrauru* relation, the absence of the *tippa-malku* wife of her *pirrauru* spouse must coincide with the absence of her own *tippa-malku* husband before this position is reached. So long as only one *tippa-malku* partner is absent, the *pirrauru* spouse is under the obligation of lightening the labours of the woman whose place she sometimes occupies, and this is very far from what we should expect in the "group marriage" stage.

On the whole therefore I conclude that the *pirrauru* relation affords absolutely no evidence of a prior stage of group marriage. So far from the quantity of evidence for group marriage having been increased by Dr Howitt's recent book, it has undergone a diminution. Gason had stated[1] that tribal brothers had the right of access in the absence of the husband without first being made *pirrauru*. This, if correct, would have been much nearer group marriage than the actual facts; the statement however appears to be incorrect, if we may judge by the fact that Dr Howitt has silently dropped it.

Of the *piraungaru* relation but little can be said, mainly for the reason that our information is so scanty. We do not learn, for example, if it is temporary or permanent, if the consent of the woman is needed, if she ever asks her husband for a certain *piraungaru*, or if she applies rather to her elder brothers. We do not know what becomes of the *piraungaru* when the primary spouse dies, whether the brother can claim a right to his brother's wife as *piraungaru* on giving presents, whether married and unmarried alike enter into the relationship, whether a woman can become *piraungaru* before she has a special husband, whether relations of free love are barred between a man and his prospective wife and permitted with other *nupa* women, and a host of other questions. We do not even learn when access is permitted to a *piraungaru* spouse. We have, it is clear, far too few data to be able to estimate the value of the dictum of Messrs Spencer and Gillen that "individual marriage does not exist either in name or in practice in the Urabunna tribe." If their views are based only on the facts they have given us, they have clearly overlooked a number of essential points; if, on the other hand, they took other facts into consideration, we may reasonably ask to be put in possession of the whole case.

[1] *Journ. Anthr. Inst.* XX, 56.

# CHAPTER XIV.

## TEMPORARY UNIONS.

Wife lending. Initiation ceremonies. *Jus primae noctis.* Punishment for adultery. *Ariltha* of central tribes. Group marriage unproven.

IT has been mentioned above that the *pirrauru* custom, so far from being an extension of the recognised practice of Australian tribes, is in some respects a limitation of it. We may now proceed to illustrate this. Even among the Dieri the tribal festival on the occasion of an inter-tribal marriage is marked by free intercourse between the sexes without regard to existing sexual unions[1] (? either *tippa-malku* or *pirrauru*). In the same way the Wiimbaio tribal gatherings were accompanied by regulated promiscuity, the class rules being the only limitation. At others wives could be lent or temporarily exchanged by the husbands[2]. The Geawe-gal held festivals at which wives were lent to young men, subject to class laws[3]. In other cases the exchange was limited to brothers or men of the same totem[4]. Among the Kamilaroi a wife was lent to friendly visitors but only with her consent. In all these cases we see a state of things similar to or not unlike the relations of the Dieri *pirrauru* spouses, and it should be noted that it is at tribal gatherings that the latter can claim to exercise their rights. From this it appears that the Dieri custom amounts to an ear-marking of certain women for the use of certain men, and is consequently a limitation of the common custom; in consideration of the fact that the *pirrauru* men protect them in the absence of their

[1] Howitt, p. 205.
[2] p. 214.
[3] p. 217.
[4] pp. 224, 260.

husbands, they are permitted at the same time to exercise marital rights, provided their own primary spouses are absent.

Among the Wiimbaio, when sickness was believed to be coming down the Murray[1], and among the Kurnai, when the *Aurora australis* was seen[2], an exchange of wives was ordered by the old men to avert the threatened evil[3]. This is explained by Dr Howitt as a reversion to the ancient custom of group marriage. It is however not quite clear on what grounds it is necessary to treat it as a survival at all. If a day of prayer and fasting is ordered in order to avert national calamities, it does not follow that the nation in question was in the habit of perpetual prayer and fasting at some previous stage of its existence. Moreover, if the magical rite was formerly the universal practice we may well ask what induced the tribes which believe in its efficacy to adopt a new form of marriage. *Ex hypothesi*, it is pleasing to Mungan, or good against disease; knowing this, they have not hesitated to abolish group marriage, but apparently without incurring Mungan's wrath, or bringing any epidemic upon them.

Among the Narrinyeri[4], the old men have a right of access to the newly initiated girls, but apparently Dr Howitt does not regard this as a survival. On the other hand the *narumbe* (initiated youths), who may not at this period take wives, had unrestricted rights over the younger women, those "of his own class and totem not excepted," and this Dr Howitt regards as a survival from the days of the undivided commune, though if it is so it is hard to see why they should have rights only over the younger women. The practice does not appear to differ from the free love found among the Dieri except in the absence of class restrictions and its limitation to the period after initiation which is among many other peoples a period of sexual licence.

Another group of customs, also interpreted by Dr Howitt as a survival of group marriage and an "expiation for individual marriage," calls for some discussion. It is unnecessary to refer here to the explanation of the *jus primae noctis* suggested by

[1] p. 195. [2] pp. 170, 277.

[3] Also among the Kurnandaburi, the Wonkamira, etc. *Journ. Anthr. Inst.* XX, 62. General circumcision was a remedy in Fiji when the chief was ill.

[4] And among the Dieri, according to Gason, *Journ. Anthr. Inst.* XX, 87.

Mr Crawley. It may be that the matter can also to some extent be explained as payment for services, in the same way as the *pirrauru* relation shows some signs of being a *quid pro quo*.

In certain tribes access to the bride is permitted to men of the group of the husband. Among the Kuinmurbura they are the men who have aided the husband to carry off the woman[1]; and the same is the case with the Kurnandaburi and Kamilaroi tribes[2]. It is very significant that among the Narrinyeri the right of access only accrues in case of elopement and precisely to those men who actually give assistance in the abduction, a fact hard to explain on the theory of expiation[3]. Among the Mukjarawaint the right seems to belong to those of the same totem, but apparently the young men only[4]; but here too their position as accessories is quite clear, as indeed it must be in any tribe where the right accrues to men of the same totem. By all the rules of savage justice a punishment may be inflicted in these cases either on the offender himself or on the men of his totem. It is therefore not strange that they require from the abductor some return for the danger to which he exposes them, especially if they actually take part in the abduction. An aberrant form of the custom is found among the Kurnai, among whom the *jus primae noctis* falls to men initiated at the same *jeraeil* as the bridegroom.

Among the Kurnandaburi there was a period of unrestricted licence after the exercise of the *jus primae noctis*, even the father of the bride being allowed access to her. This did not of course violate totem or phratry regulations. Dr Howitt does not comment on the case, but it would have been interesting to hear whether both these customs are to be regarded as survivals and if so what caused the duplication[5].

In estimating the value of the custom of *jus primae noctis* as evidence of a prior state of group marriage, a custom of the Yuin should not be overlooked. If a man elopes with another man's

[1] p. 219. [2] pp. 205, 193. *J. A. I.* XII, 36.
[3] p. 245. [4] p. 269.
[5] He also omits to mention the *Muni* ceremony, described in *Journ. Anthr. Inst.* XX, 62. If general licence is of magical efficacy in cases of sickness, it can hardly be argued that general licence at marriage has not, as Mr Crawley argues, a magical significance.

betrothed he is punished by having to fight the girl's father, brothers, and mother's brother; the girl was sometimes punished by being beaten; all the men who pursued her had a right of access provided they were of the right totem and locality. If however the eloping couple were not caught they were not liable to punishment after a child was born. There is no mention of any *jus primae noctis* where the marriage was the result of betrothal. In this case therefore the right of access is a punishment, so far as the girl is concerned; it is earned by taking part in the pursuit, a fact which confirms the suggested explanation of the right of access at marriage.

It should not be overlooked that this form of punishment is found among some tribes as the penalty for adultery[1], when it certainly cannot be interpreted as an expiation for individual marriage. This was the case among the Wotjoballuk, the Kamilaroi, and the Euahlayi.

We may now turn to the customs of the central and northern tribes visited by Messrs Spencer and Gillen. Except in the case of three of the north-eastern tribes the right of access accrues in connection with the *ariltha* ceremony. It may be said at once that there is among these tribes no trace of access as payment for services; for on the rare occasions when a wife is captured she is allotted to an individual and becomes his property at once, according to a statement in the first work of Spencer and Gillen[2]. In the same work, it is true, this statement is contradicted by the assertion that on such occasions only the men of the right class are allowed to have access[3]. But this statement does not seem to be based on any facts within the knowledge of the writers, for they make a definite statement to the contrary with regard to the Arunta customs, and it was with the Arunta that they were specially concerned, and in the later volume no further details are given, as they should have been, if the custom was found among any of the tribes visited on the second expedition.

The association of the right of access with the initiation ceremony is paralleled, as we have already seen, among other tribes. It hardly seems necessary to argue a state of primitive

[1] p. 245. [2] *C. T.* 556. [3] *C. T.* 104.

promiscuity from a custom of licence at the period of puberty, which does not in fact differ, except in degree, from the licence normally enjoyed by the unmarried, and is readily explicable on other grounds than those suggested by Spencer and Gillen. If we are not prepared to regard this licence at puberty, which may equally well have subsisted side by side with marriage or group promiscuity, as a mere expression of the newly attained sexual rights, we have as an alternative the magical theory of Mr Crawley. I do not propose to dwell on this but will pass at once to discuss some points which seem to have escaped the notice of Spencer and Gillen when they proposed their hypothesis of promiscuity.

The essential point in connection with these ceremonies is the fact that access is not limited, as in the case of the Dieri, to men who might lawfully marry the woman. The right is restricted to men of six classes out of the eight, including all four of the other moiety and the two of her own half of her own moiety. Now whatever else may be deduced from this, one thing is clear, and that is that the custom in its present form, at any rate, took its rise before the eight classes were introduced but after the four classes were already in existence and *a fortiori* after the phratries were known. Consequently no argument for promiscuity can be founded on the right of access at initiation. It cannot be a survival from a time when no marriage regulations were known, for the simple reason that the custom itself bears unmistakeable traces of regulations of a comparatively advanced type. It may of course be argued that these limitations are of late origin. How far this is so and why such limitations should have been introduced it is impossible to say; but it is impossible to base an argument for primitive promiscuity on a state of things which is admittedly not primitive unless we have good *primâ facie* grounds for regarding the custom as a survival. There is nothing in the present case to show that it is not a magical rite.

At other times access is permitted in accordance with class regulations, the husband's consent being necessary, if indeed he does not actually take the preliminary steps himself. We have seen that a similar state of things exists in other tribes.

It does not seem necessary to look for the explanation further than the ordinary customs of savage hospitality, the desire to do a favour to men who may be useful. It is difficult to see why Spencer and Gillen regard the fact that women are lent in this way only to their *unawa* as a proof of the former existence of group marriage. Clearly if intercourse is permitted only between certain persons before marriage and only certain persons are allowed to marry, we can hardly be surprised to find that these latter are restricted in the choice of men to whom they may lend their wives after marriage. The surprising thing would be if it were otherwise.

In addition, as in the tribes we have already considered, irregular access is practised for magical purposes in connection with the performance of ceremonies and the sending out of messengers. It has already been pointed out that we have no grounds for regarding such practices as survivals; for if we put on sackcloth and ashes as a penance for our misdeeds, it does not follow that this was ever the prevailing costume. It is even less possible to interpret the ritual lending of wives to messengers as a survival, for, *ex hypothesi*, the messengers were not of the group which "group-married," and messengers of any sort point to a stage when inter-tribal relations had made considerable advance and the tribes in question are hardly likely to have been still in the stage of the "undivided commune."

The survey of Australian customs and terms of relationship leads us to the conclusion that the former, so far from proving the present or even former existence of group marriage in that continent, do not even render it probable; on the latter no argument of any sort can be founded which assumes them to refer to consanguinity, kinship or affinity. It is therefore not rash to say that the case for group marriage, so far as Australia is concerned, falls to the ground. Even were it otherwise, even were group marriage proved for Australia or for any other part of the world, we should still be far from having established promiscuity and group marriage as a stage in the general history of mankind. For that at least a scheme of development is needed. Even were the arguments in favour of the group marriage hypothesis much stronger, its supporters might reasonably be asked to give us something more than assertion and reassertion without any attempt to show in detail the process of evolution. To take an example from another sphere, it may safely be said that the general theory of evolution would find few supporters if it were not possible to trace some existing species and genera back to some generalised type in the past. At present the position of a supporter of the theory of primitive promiscuity and group marriage is analogous to that of an evolutionist who can only point to a few more or less useless peculiarities in the anatomy of man without being able to show resemblances between them and the corresponding portions of fossil or actually existing anthropoids. He calls them "vestiges[1]" and insists that *homo* is descended from a generalised anthropoid. The mere assertion of the vestigial character of such bones or organs would hardly carry conviction unless they could be shown to exist in some anthropoid in a more fully developed state. Similarly the arguments for promiscuity and group marriage suffer from incurable weakness, and would so suffer, even were the basis far more reliable than I have shown to be the case, unless and until it has been shown by what process and for what reasons man took each upward step. So far only one writer has attempted, and that nearly thirty years ago, to trace the course of human development on the hypothesis of primitive promiscuity, and his scheme is a house of cards.

The student of sociology is at a disadvantage compared with the zoologist in not being able to unearth his fossils for comparison with living forms. He must therefore trace the relationship between living forms, and, in seeking to discover the earlier stages of human progress, rely in part on the sociology of the higher mammals, in part on the possibility of showing a logical scheme of human development. When he examines the living forms he is of course unable to say whether actually existing savage institutions are in the main line of human progress or merely bye-paths embryological or teratological. It may be

[1] Commonly but erroneously termed "rudimentary organs." It is a natural and justifiable assumption for a zoologist that all vestigial organs have previously been more largely developed. It is also an assumption that a given custom is vestigial, but it is not a justifiable one.

possible to show that group marriage exists somewhere on the earth at the present time. Even if this is so, the theory of primitive promiscuity and group marriage as stages in the general history of mankind remain mere baseless guesses until we have a systematic account both of the causes which led to the various steps, and of the processes by which the various stages were reached.

# APPENDIX.

## ANOMALOUS MARRIAGES.

Decay of class rules in South-East. Descent in Central Tribes. "Bloods" and "Castes."

A CERTAIN number of Australian tribes have ceased to adhere strictly to the regulations of their class systems. Thus, in the Kamilaroi tribe a correspondent of Dr Howitt's found intra-class marriage, the totem only being different; in determining the class and totem of the children the ordinary rule held good[1]. The Wiradjeri on the Lachlan permit Ipai to marry Muri as well as Kumbo, the two classes both belonging to Kupathin; in each case certain totems only, viz. emu, opossum, snake and bandicoot, have the privilege[2]. The same anomaly is found in the Wonghibon tribe[3].

Among the Warramunga and other northern tribes Spencer and Gillen find that the division of the classes, explained in the last chapter, does not prevent marriages from taking place which this division ought to prevent, if the Arunta rule were followed[4]. A curious feature of these marriages is that the children of the anomalous union pass into the class which would have been theirs if their mother had wedded her normal spouse. It is not easy to say whether this should be regarded as a survival of matrilineal descent; it is, however, clear that only the existence of phratriac names enables us to say definitely that the descent in this tribe is in the male line.

According to the information printed by Mr R. H. Mathews this irregularity is by no means the sum total of anomalies.

[1] Howitt, p. 204.
[2] *ib.* p. 211.
[3] *ib.* p. 214, cf. *J. A. I.*
[4] *Nor. Tr.* pp. 107, 114.

His information is far from being commonly accepted as accurate; but, as will be shown later, there are correspondences between his statements and those of other observers, which make it probable that his statements have some basis in fact. At any rate they deserve notice, if only that they may be contradicted by competent witnesses, if they are incorrect.

In the Inchalachee tribe, according to Mr Mathews, descent of the classes is reckoned through females. In the place of the arrangement shown in Table I a, he gives the order 3, 4, 8, 7; 6, 5, 1, 2[1]. Any man of the first moiety may marry any woman of the second, though certain marriages are normal and one of the remainder more usual than the others. The effect of these rules is to make it possible for a man to marry any woman of his own generation, even if she be of his own class. This is precisely the same as the case reported from the Kamilaroi by Dr Howitt, if we may take it that in the latter case the normal marriages are found side by side with the anomalous ones.

In the Inchalachee marriages the children, as in the Warramunga cases of Spencer and Gillen, take the class which they would have had if the woman had taken her normal spouse. On this Mr Mathews relies for the statement that descent is reckoned in the female line in this tribe. But, as we have seen, such a view is erroneous as regards the Warramunga, among whom anomalous marriages also occur; it is therefore by no means clear that the Inchalachee are matrilineal. We have even more reason to doubt his view as to the Binbinga, for whom we have the evidence of Spencer and Gillen.

Mr Mathews also reports among the Wiradjeri marriages resembling in many respects those mentioned above from the Wailwun tribe[2]. The table does not seem to be complete; it is therefore useless to enquire on what principle these marriages are arranged. There seems, however, no reason to doubt the substantial accuracy of the information.

More revolutionary is the statement that these cross-class marriages are based on an actual kinship organisation, to which Mr Mathews gives the name of "blood" (Table III, p. 50)[3].

1 *Proc. R. G. S. Qu.* XX, 71.

2 *J. R. S. N. S. W.* XXXI, 173.

3 *ib.* XXXVIII, 207–17, XXXIX, 117, *Proc. R. G. S. Qu.* XX, 53, etc.

Running across the phratries and classes are divisions known as Gwaigullean and Gwaimudthen, Muggulu and Bumbirra, etc., which have the meaning of "sluggish" and "swift" blood respectively. The bloods again are sometimes subdivided. In the Ngeumba tribe Gwaimudthen is divided into nhurai (butt) and wangue (middle), while Gwaigulir is equivalent to winggo (top). These names refer to different portions of the shadow of a tree and refer to the positions taken up in camping by the persons belonging to the different "bloods" and "castes." In this, it may be noted, these organisations follow the parallel of the phratries and classes.

With the correspondences in names shown in Table III. before our eyes, it is difficult to suppose that the statements of Mr Mathews have no basis in fact. In the absence of further information, however, it is clearly impossible to discuss the origin of these divisions. It seems most probable that they are the systematisation of the anomalous marriages already cited. But much more information is needed before anything like certainty can be attained in the matter. Both actual genealogies and tables of terms of relationship must be in our hands before we can come to a decision.

# INDEX OF PHRATRY, BLOOD, AND CLASS NAMES.

Phratry and Blood names are in caps., Class names in roman. In the references Map II is equivalent to Table I (pp. 42—48), Map III to Table II (pp. 48—51). The numbers refer to pages, save in the case of Table I a.

# SUBJECT INDEX.

Names of Australian tribes are in Clarendon, native words and parts of words in italics. Words in inverted commas are defined.

CAMBRIDGE: PRINTED BY JOHN CLAY, M.A. AT THE UNIVERSITY PRESS.

For EU product safety concerns, contact us at Calle de José Abascal, 56–1°, 28003 Madrid, Spain or eugpsr@cambridge.org.

www.ingramcontent.com/pod-product-compliance
Ingram Content Group UK Ltd.
Pitfield, Milton Keynes, MK11 3LW, UK
UKHW012343130625
459647UK00009B/490

* 9 7 8 1 1 0 8 0 1 0 5 1 1 *